Headin' for the Rhubarb!

A New Hampshire Dictionary (well, kinda)

More Funny Stuff from Islandport Press

Live Free and Eat Pie! A Storyteller's Guide to New Hampshire
By Rebecca Rule

Down the Road a Piece: A Storyteller's Guide to Maine
By John McDonald

Not Too Awful Bad: A Storyteller's Guide to Vermont
By Leon Thompson

The Best of Bert and I (CD)
By Marshall Dodge and Robert Bryan

Bert and I On Stage: Marshall Dodge Live (CD)
By Marshall Dodge

A Moose and a Lobster Walk into a Bar...
By John McDonald

Visit www.islandportpress.com for a complete list of
our books and CDs

Headin' for the Rhubarb!

A New Hampshire Dictionary (well, kinda)

by Rebecca Rule

ISLANDPORT PRESS

YARMOUTH • MAINE

Islandport Press
P.O. Box 10
Yarmouth, Maine 04096

www.islandportpress.com

ISBN: 978-1-934031-44-5
Library of Congress Control Number: 2010936232

First edition published September 2010

Book design by Michelle Lunt / Islandport Press
Cover Design by Karen Hoots / Mad Hooter Design

For Arthur Slade, good friend, first reader, and big help.

Acknowledgments

Many kind people contributed words, expressions, place names, and stories. Some I met at storytelling sessions around the state. These were held at libraries, town halls, historical societies, opera houses, community theaters, and churches—many sponsored by the New Hampshire Humanities Council. I scribbled stories down as best I could, but didn't always catch the names of the tellers. Thank you to the Humanities Council and to these generous, anonymous contributors. You wouldn't be anonymous if I wasn't such a featherhead.

Some people wrote letters or e-mails, called, or told stories when I was taking good notes, so I did catch a few names. Thanks to Roland Aube, Joann Bailey, Martha Barrett, Phyllis Bennett, Gordon Blakeney, Eileen Brown, Janet Brown, Jennie Brown, Roger Brown, Helen Burns, Normand Caouette, John Chandler, Phil Chapman, Dave Colquitt, Caleb Corriveau, Fred Creed, Michael J. Curtiss, Justine Dodge, Don and Ann Dollard, Sarah Earle, Neil English, Grace Enman, Mike Faiella, Mary Farmer, Alden and Olive Farrar, Josephine Fearon, Susan Ware Flower, Loisanne Foster, Bill Gleed, Betty Gordon, Norman Greene, David Griffin, Daniel Webster Harvey, Ada and Urban Hatch, Michelle Hernandez, Anita Hickey, Joey Holmes, David Howard, Ginger Jannenga, Dick Jarvis, Vea Jenks, Cheryl Johnson, Don Johnson, Martha Jordan, Roberta Kallum, Tom Keegan, Ruth Keith, Roger Kelly, Bob Kent, Marion Knox, Jean Lane, Cindy Larmie, Odette LeClerc, Steve Lombard, Bob Lovely, Ernest Mack, Buddy McDougall, Dick Merrill, Jeff Miller, Sheree Miller, Smokey Miller, Nancy Nelson, Howard Odell, Fred and Mary Jane Ogmundson, Norma Oleson, Ola Oleson, Peg Osterman, Mildred Otto, Steve Pruyne, George Radcliffe, Bob Ramsay, Kenneth Reid, Lisa Rollins, Perry Sawyer, David Smallidge, John Scudder, Frumie Selchen, Joel Sherburne, Sue Ann Sidell, Medora

Snigger, Gracia Snyder, Mary Stuart, Virginia Stuart, Olive Tardiff, Harvey Tolman, Kendra Totman, Katie Towler, and Walter Walker.

And thanks to those who suggested words, expressions, and place names when I sounded the call, including: Carol Anderson, Marilyn Arsenau, Carol Bagan, Kent Barker, Kathleen Battles-Burden, Barbara Benn, George Bozeman, Chip Brindamour, Katy Brown, Mary Brown, Deb Bruss, Rick Brussard, Amy Cane, Rhoda Capron, Kristina Carlson, Mike Cornog, Peter Crane, Alden Dill, Martha Donovan, Ed Fayle, Stanley Ford, Glynis Gordon, Carol Gregory, Martin Gross, Muffie Henderson, Jere Henley, Becky Keating, Bob Kent, David Killam, Kathy Lacroix, Jeff Lalish, Ron Letourneau, Elizabeth Longfellow, Nancy Macy, Lesley Marquis, Chip Noon, Eric Pinder, Barbara Potvin, Andy Robert, Chuck Sink, Kathy Smith, Tracey Rauh Solomon, Trudy Sutherland, Diane Tebbetts, Bill Twombley, Linda Tyring, Lauren Verge, Scott Vignault, Charter Weeks, and Mimi White.

North Country stories were collected for the Telling Our Stories project, sponsored by the Androscoggin Community Partners, including the Arts Alliance of Northern New Hampshire, the Family Resource Center at Gorham, N.H., and the United Way. Funding for that project came from the New Hampshire State Council on the Arts, the New Hampshire Humanities Council, and Public Service of New Hampshire. Thanks to the sponsors of that project and to the many participants who gave their time and their stories.

Special thanks also to my parents, Lewis and Jean Barker, for raising me in a home so rich with language.

Dean Lunt, Amy Canfield, Trudy Price, and all the folks at Islandport Press—a sincere thank-you for this opportunity and your contagious enthusiasm.

And, finally, thanks to John Rule, Adi Rule, and K Seavey—my weird little nuclear family of ahtists—for putting up with me.

A Take on Talk

The native New Hampshire accent combines the stretched As of Maaassachusetts, the dropped Rs of Maine, and the hint of *oi* and *ew* so pronounced in Vermont expressions like "Boi gawd, that's some hansome kew." (Translation: Golly gosh, that's a good-looking Holstein). We drop some consonants and add others. Why? Because that's the way it's always been done. (The preceding, by the way, is one our favorite expressions, also used to explain the inefficiencies of town and state government.) A distinguishing characteristic is the migrating R. It travels from one word to another. Idea becomes idear while supper turns to suppa and mother morphs into muhtha, as in "Beans and brown bread for suppa? Good idear, Muhtha."

Someone from away might say: Lisa Miner drove her Ford pickup to Norman's House of Pizza and Seafood, where she enjoyed a meal of lobster with drawn butter, buns, and corn.

We'd say: Liser Mina drove her Fo-ahd pickup to Nahmin's House of Peetzer and Seafood, where she enjoyed a meal of lobstah with drawn buttah, buns, and con.

Note how the R in Miner hopped to the end of Lisa and the one in Norman slid over into pizza, rounding those words out nicely.

Note also, that the R in Ford disappeared, allowing two syllables in place of one. We enjoy syllables, which is why words that have just one in some parts of the country get stretched into two around he-ah, as in grossry sto-ah or Budweiser be-ah. Again, reluctant to waste a thing, we borrow the extra syllable from elsewhere, which is why grocery turns to grossry. It's tit for tat. Tricky, but not hahd to figure once you see the pattun. For example, Gs. We drop them from the ends of words ending in *ing*, but leave them alone otherwise. "Maggie dug the hole, all right, but in the diggin' strained a muscle in her back, and she's been complainin' ever since."

The accent varies from region to region, town to town, family to family, person to person. People from away say, "Nobody talks like that anymore." They say, "The old New Hampshire is long gone." Granted, nobody uses all the pronunciations or expressions cited here. Nobody ever did. But a good many of them live on in the language of people from small towns—or big towns that used to be small. The accent is strong among members of historical societies, women's clubs, men's clubs, and farm bureaus. It comes right back at me when I speak to retired teachers, septage haulers, elk farmers, Lions Club members, Blue Cross retirees, health-care professionals, and caregivers. I hear it at assisted-living facilities and grand hotels. I even hear it at schools. As one little girl said, "You talk just like my nana." And a little bit like you, too, I thought.

The old New Hampshire is not long gone. You just have to know where to look and listen for it. The accent lives on even as it changes. Language is always changing; that's what makes it so frickin' innerestin'.

One thing for shoe-uh, our particular incarnation is hahd to imitate. This book is not intended to teach you how to talk like a native. Fritz Wetherbee put out a CD for that purpose. It's called *Speak N'Hamsha Like a Native*. Fritz, a seventh-generation native and television personality, knows his stuff. You are welcome to go ahead and try the accent, but many have tried before, and hardly anybody gets it right. Hollywood actors do French accents, Russian accents, Jamaican and Minnesotan accents like nobody's business. But when they try ours, it sounds like a cross between Texas and County Cork (pronounced County Cock). Even Fritz will admit, you kinda hafta be bawn to it.

Not that a lot of actors even attempt the New Hampshire accent; they primarily attempt to talk like Mainers. From Hollywood, evidently, northern New England appears to be one big state, heavily forested and populated primarily by moose and lobstuh. Folks from away—I do not tell a lie—have said to me: "Maine, New Hampshire, Vermont—pretty much all the same. Right?"

Uh, wrong.

A dissertation on the differences among the northern New England states, that's a whole nutha book. (Whole nutha—now there's a New Hampshire expression. I wouldn't have thought of it, except my daughter, who is much smarter than me—has been since she was 13 years old—once said, "Muhtha, nutha is not a word."

"'Scuse, me," I said. "I meant to say, whole nuth-err."

"Muhtha," she said, "nuth-err is not a word either."

Smart-ass, I thought. But I didn't say it because she's bigger than me (and meaner).

Generally speaking, the New Hampshire cadence is swifter than the Maine drawl. Gawd, those Mainuhs take a long time to plow through a story. Although, if you recorded a Mainuh at 33 ⅓ rpms and played him back at 78, you'd get something like a New Hampshire accent. Our enunciation is more British than the Mainuh's, but less British than those Maaassachusetts fellows with their Haarvaard gutturals and shiny caahs in well-maintained yaahds. Plus we spend less time talking about lobstuh, beans, bluebrys, podaydahs, and maple syrup than folks in neighboring states. We enjoy all those northern New England delicacies, but we're not obsessed with 'em. Politics? Maybe. Taxes? Definitely.

I've been practicing the New Hampshire accent, listening to it, and collecting New Hampshire expressions all my life (so far). In Part One of this book, which makes up the bulk of it, you'll find words, sayings, pronunciations, examples, and stories. That's the Dictionary section. In the Gazetteer section, you'll find place names and references, so if you end up in Boscawen or Westmoreland, you'll have some idea where you are and how to say so. I've included a few stories and a little history in that section as well. Couldn't resist. You know that old theory about how the Earth rests on the shell of a giant turtle? And that turtle's standing on the shell of another. The child asks: "What's holding up that second turtle?" And the sage says, "It's turtles all the way down." For me, it's stories all the way down.

No doubt I've missed some biggies in the language department and made some glaring mistakes, but maybe you'll write me a letter, send an e-mail, or give me a call to let me know so I can make corrections in the next edition (should there be one). Thanks in advance for that.

Of course, there's no such thing as pure New Hampshire talk. Naturally, there's spillage back and forth over the borders of other New England states. Who knows—some of the expressions that I think are exclusively New Hampshire might pop up in West Virginia, Nebraska, or California. People travel and so does the language. In other words, no guarantees.

If you're from New Hampshire, maybe you'll recognize yourself, your relations, or your neighbors. If you're from away, maybe these explanations will help you understand the state, its language, and its people a little better. Maybe then you won't make the mistake of strutting into a general store and asking for a large frost heave to go.

Here we go. In alphabetical order . . .

Dictionary

A

Abenaki

Early human inhabitants of New Hampshire

Abenaki, roughly, means people of the dawn land, so it seemed like a fitting first word for this dictionary. First word, first light.

able to be up and about and partake of nourishment

Not bad, considering

Answers the question, "How you doing?"

Other answers: "Can't complain; nobody listens." Or, "Pretty good considering what I been through."

Which prompts the question: "What is it you been through, Stanley?"

To which Stanley replies, "Well, the last thing was a set of stayahs."

accommodatin'

Aiming to please

Kendra Totman's dad found an accommodatin' storekeeper just off the pike on his way to Hanover. He was hauling a trailer that got to banging around behind him, and, when he pulled over to see what was wrong, he realized one of the bolts had fallen out. He walked down the road and located the bolt, but it was bent and useless.

He left the trailer in the ditch and drove to the next exit. In the village, he found a country store.

Accommodatin' fella says, "Can I help you?"

"Do you have a hardware section?"

"Ayuh. Back of the store."

"Do you have some pliers?"

"Ayuh, we got ply-uhs. Here you go."

"How about a wrench?"

"Yup."

"Do you happen to have any bolts like this one?" He held up the bent bolt from the trailer.

"Nope," the fella said. "We only got straight ones."

ache-ridge

Land

The more ache-ridge you have, the more aches and pains you'll get perambulating the bounds, near as you can figure them from deeds that say "more or less" (with confidence) and often reference corner markers like "the big crooked elm" or "the rock young Chester climbed on to escape the bear."

across the pond

Across the Atlantic

If your boat out of New Castle misses the Isles of Shoals in the fog, next thing you know you'll be sailing across the pond and end up in Portugal. Some also refer to the pond as the big drink of water.

a-crowdin'

Getting too close

Ruth Keith drove out to visit a friend. On the dirt road, a few miles from the friend's house, Ruth noticed a recently built Cape, the only other house on the road. When Ruth asked her friend about her new neighbors, the country lady said: "Yup, they's a-crowdin' me."

aggravatin'

Bothersome

Driving home to Lebanon from Concord, Rick was caught in a big snowstorm. He got behind a line of cars slow as turtles on I-89—timid and just crawling along—which Rick found aggravatin'. So he pulled into the passing lane in his big-ass four-wheel-drive and commenced to pass. He passed 10 cars, 20 cars, 50 cars. When he finally got to the head of the line, he looked over to see who was setting the snail's pace. It was his brother.

agin

Used by some old-timers instead of against

In the North County, a man retired from the school board having served more than 45 years. When asked if he'd seen a lot of changes in schools during his tenure, he said, "I have. And I was agin 'em all."

a-go-in'

Moving, active

The Energizer bunny in those cute commercials keeps a-go-in' and a-go-in' and a-go-in'.

ah

Pronounced as in "Open your mouth and say ah"

1. *It's a homonym for both are and our, which can be confusing.*

At storytelling sessions, I've been known to say, "Ah stories ah ah identity," then translate if people look puzzled. "Our stories are our identity." Which they answer, "Ah, ahcowuss."

2. The 18th letter of the alphabet

Gave me a lot of trouble as a kid, since my maiden name was Barker, which I pronounce Bahkah. I learned to explain it to people by spelling it out: "My name's Becky Bahkah, B-A-ah-K-E-ah." That seemed to clear things up.

ahcowuss

Naturally; goes without saying

Sometimes used ironically, as in: "Brock never lies. Neither, ahcowuss, do those politicians up the State House." You could say, up to the State House, but why wouldja?

ahold

When you contact someone, especially by telephone, you get ahold of them

"Did you get ahold of Geraldine last night?"

"Finally! She's on a pahty line. Every time I dialed her up, her neighbor Rufus answered. I said, 'Rufus, how come you keep picking up when it's not your ring?' "

"He says, 'Phone rings. I answer it.' "

aht

Paintings, sculptures, writings, music, and so forth

Frank Case recalls a Raymond school meeting where it was put to a vote whether to hire a part-time aht teacher. After much discussion, a voter said with conviction, "Raymond ain't never had no Pikahtzo, and it ain't never gonna have no Pikahtzo."

"Not if you don't hire an aht teacher, it ain't."

ain't

Am not, is not

Alphonse got stopped for driving too slow. The officer asked why he was going 29 in a 50-mile-per-hour zone.

Alphonse said: "I ain't going nowhere. Ain't no one waiting for me. And I ain't in no hurry."

ain't much fetchin' up he-ah

Better go get what you want because it's not going to come floating in with the tide

At the church supper, we sat politely looking at our empty plates while others lined up at the buffet. Finally, Mary said: "Better get in line. Ain't much fetchin' up he-ah."

airear

A place

"Jake claimed he spotted Bigfoot up on Tucker Mountain. We dint believe him at first, but sure enough, we spotted some strange tracks in that same airear when we were out bird huntin'. Kinda gave me the willies."

Note: Not to be confused with ah-REE-ahs. If your payments are late, your mortgage might fall into ah-REE-ahs.

all set

As a question, all set means "Do you have what you need?" As an answer, it means "I'm fine for the moment, but come back in a few minutes; I might need a refill on my coffee."

So a conversation might go like this:
"All set?"
"All set."
"You shoe-uh?"
"Ayup."

all tolled

1. Church bells ring to signal that one of our own has passed.

One toll for a man. Two for a woman. Followed, according to tradition, by a toll for every year the person lived. For an octogenarian, that would be more than 80 tolls, all tolled.

2. The sum total, accumulated cost

"Between insurance, registration, and the new transmission, that free cah cost me over a thousand dollars, all tolled."

3. The fee you pay to use the New Hampshire Turnpike

Tolls go to pay for road maintenance. Which explains all those orange cones, bottlenecks, and state employees along the side of the road working hard—except for the vice presidents in charge of the heavy lookin'-on.

And then there's the mystery of those signs warning of a work area ahead, slow down, fines doubled. So you keep a-go-in'. The turnpike narrows to one lane. Traffic creeps. You pass 200 orange cones, but nobody's working on the road. No equipment. No nothing. Not even a hole in the ground. What the heck is that about?

I'll tell you what that's about. A surplus of orange cones.

It's the New Hampshire way. If you got 'em, you gotta use 'em.

People used to pay a nickel toll for the privilege of crossing the bridge connecting Springfield, Vermont, and Charlestown, New Hampshire. Gary pulled up to the booth behind a Cadillac with New York (pronounced *New Yawk*) plates. This was fairly late at night and Gary was anxious to get home, but there was some kind of holdup. In the lit-up booth, he saw the collector rummaging around in drawers (pronounced *draws*). Then the collector left the booth and walked across the road to a house—presumably his. Lights went on and off, one after another, room to room, upstairs and down, as the collector passed through. Ten minutes later, he emerged, walked back across the road to the booth, and handed something to the driver of the Cadillac with New York plates. The Cadillac moved on. Gary pulled up to the window.

"What was that all about?" he asked.

"Well," the toll keeper said, "that guy from New York handed me a hundred dollar bill. Guess he didn't think I'd take it and bother to make change."

amongst the missin'

Lost

"My fishing hat seems to be amongst the missin'."

"You mean that ragged, ratty, stinky old thing that looks like a dead frog on your head?"

"Yeah, you seen it?"

"If I had I wouldn't say so."

Roland Aube tells of his father, Delphine, who once won a trophy for second prize in a hoss-pulling contest at the Lancaster Fair. Afterwards, whenever company came to the house, Delphine would pull out his trophy and tell the rather lengthy story of how he came to win it. Until one day, he went to collect the trophy where he thought he'd left it and it was amongst the missin'. "Maybe it's up in the attic," he said, "or down cellah. Or maybe Muhtha tucked it in the back of the closet."

The trophy never showed up again.

After Delphine died, Roland and his brother were taking down a shed on the property that had previously been an outhouse. They got the building down and the lumber cleared away and were digging around in the rich soil underneath, when they hit something with the shovel. *Clink!* They dug down and there was the trophy.

They cleaned it off and took it up to the house.

"Muhtha," they said, "look!"

"Oh," she said tahtly, "you found it."

ample sufficiency
Enough

At the end of a meal, someone might ask, "Have you had enough to eat?"

Someone might answer: "I've had ample sufficiency. Anything more would be anathema to my delicate constitution."

At the table Grandma asked if everyone had enjoyed sufficiency. The little grandson said, "I dint know there was any."

and them
The others

"Ursula and them are coming by camp on Tuesday for a dip."

apple jack
A strong apple drink

Sweet cider is made from apples squished and strained. Hard cider is sweet cider fermented. Apple jack is hard cider frozen, and what little doesn't freeze—the almost-pure alcohol—drained and drunk.

Drunk being the operative word.

asafetida bag

A medicine bag worn around the neck, filled with herbs to ward off germs

Say it aloud it few times. It's fun. Kind of a one-word poim.

"What's that you've got hanging around your neck?"

"My asafetida bag. A cue-ah for the common cold."

"Ain't that wonderful?"

"Not so's you'd notice." *Sniff.*

ass over teakettle

Dramatic tumble

An ass-over-teakettle fall may involve a somersault, back flip, butt slide, or all of the above.

"Heard you went through a set of stayahs, Stanley."

"Ayup. Virginia sent me down cellah for a jah of gerkins. Stepped on a rotten bo-ahd and down I went, ass over teakettle."

"Get hurt?"

"Dint do me any good."

My grandfather, Trapper Bill Barker, at age 90 or so, got it into his head to cut his firewood on a steep hill at the back of his property. One week, when we visited, he was pretty stove up, having slipped and rolled ass over teakettle to the bottom of the hill.

Through the summer and fall, he kept us apprised of his progress on his woodpile: 10 wheelbarrow loads, 20, 50, whatever it was. "Don't kill yourself working on that wood, Grampa," we told him.

"Kill myself! It's what's keeping me alive."

When he died at 92, the woodpile stretched longer than his house. 'Course, he lived in a two-room cabin—three if you count the attached outhouse.

assparograss

Asparagus

"If you don't keep the assparograss patch weeded, the little ass-parograsses will get choked out."

Or, as Miss Purty at the assisted-living facility said of the vegetable served at dinner, "Assparograss again! I hate assparograss! It scours me right out."

aunt

Relative; father's or mother's sister

In this case we say the word just like it's spelled, or, in some places, with an R in the middle for good measure: arent. We all agree, however, that an aunt is not an ant. Ants live in hills and the red ones bite. My aunt is my mother's or father's sister. Either that or she's married to my mother's or father's brother.

A woman who lived in the mountains told how her aunt from the flatlands paid a visit. When Auntie went to watch her favorite program one evening, she discovered that the channel for her favorite program didn't come in. Nothing but static.

"Next time I visit," Auntie said, "I'll bring my own TV."

ayah

1. What we breathe

2. To freshen by hanging outside

"I'm going to put this musty blanket on the line and ayah it out."

ayuh

All-purpose positive (but mildly noncommittal) response

Some of us use it a lot, some not at all, some only when talking to people from away—who find the word, for some reason, entertaining.

The fella from away asks the native: "Do you know how to get to New Boston?"

"Ayuh."

Note: Ayuh can be pronounced many different ways, carrying just as many different meanings. It can express surprise, dismay, anger, affection, disapproval, approval, concern—and that's just for starters. Use with caution. Or better yet, refrain from using it at all unless you know what you're doing.

ayup

Combines ayuh and yup; a cheery affirmative

"Heard you won the Megabucks."

"Ayup."

B

back fawty

Plot of land some distance from the house

The fawty (40) is approximate; could be any amount of ache-ridge, from 2 to 100. A 100-acre farm in New Hampshire is considered substantial. We are a small state.

Fella from Texas asked a New Hampshire dairy farmer the size of his spread. (They call farms "spreads" in Texas.)

"Do you see those hills beyond the field?" the farmer said. "That's the end of my property."

"On my spread in Texas, I can drive my truck all day and into the night and still be on my own land," the fella said.

"Ayuh," the dairy farmer said, "I got a truck like that, too."

bahn

A large wooden building to shelter farm animals and store hay, tools, and tractors

Leroy was manning the vegetable stand down by the road at Harmony Farm. Truck pulls up. "How much you getting for mulch hay?" the driver asks.

"Dollah a bale," Leroy says. "Go ahead and drive right up to the bahn, the old man's there now."

The old man loads ten bales into the truck. "That'll be twelve dollars and fifty cents."

"Leroy said it was a dollah a bale."

"Ain't Leroy's hay."

At the Robert Frost House in Derry, a Midwesterner expressed his amazement to manager Bill Gleed that the bahn was attached to the house. "Why don't you folks put your barns out in the field where they belong?"

Bill said, "February."

bahth

Immersion in a tub of soapy water

Sue from Seabrook said the folks from North Seabrook didn't mix much with the folks from South Seabrook where she grew up. Her mother claimed the North Seabrookers were snots. They talked fancy for one thing. Instead of glass, they said glahss. Instead of basket, they said bahsket. They were just putting on ayahs and there was no need of it. Then she'd call Sue in from playing outside: "Come in now, Sue, and take your bahth."

Baldwins

A taht, hahd apple

Fred Creed's brother was a pie aficionado. (Who among us is not?) Viola asked him how he liked the pie she'd made special for him. He said, " 'T'would've been better if you'd used Baldwins."

McIntosh apples are another favorite. And Cortlands. (Pronounced *Cawtlins*.)

banded

The banding of the roads hails mud season.

Ginger Jannenga says one of the first signs of spring in the North Country is when the roads get banded—that is, signs go up limiting the tonnage of trucks passing that way. Some of these back roads get soft and mucky. The heavy trucks sink right down, and it takes a tractor to get 'em out. Of course, if the tractor gets stuck, you're up to your neck in it.

As the old story goes, Clint is setting on his porch in mud season when he spots a hat in the road. Oddly, the hat seems to be moving. Then he sees a head under the hat. It's the postman, Ham Hillsgrove. "Ham," Clint says. "I guess the mud's pretty deep. You seem to be up to your neck in it."

"Bettah b'lieve it," Ham says. "And I'm on hossback."

In Northwood, a traveler got his vehicle stuck in a mud hole on a back road. Luckily, it was right in front of a house. He knocked and the owner agreed to pull the vehicle out with his tractor for $10. After the vehicle was freed, the owner said: "Seems like I spend half my time pulling vehicles out of that mud hole!"

"What do you do the other half of the time?" the traveler asked.

"Haul water."

bass after a June bug
Quickly and with enthusiasm

"Ninety-five in the shade. I offered Winnie a cold Sam Adams and she went for it like a bass after a June bug."

bateau
A flat-bottomed boat

Bateaus were used to transport loggers on the rivers as they guided floating pulpwood from the woods to the mill.

Asked whether it was dangerous being raised in the logging camps, Medora Snigger said: "My mother gave us a good scare once."

To cross the Androscoggin, workers rigged a bateau on cables and pulleys. A person could go from one side of the river to the other by standing in the bateau and pulling on the cables.

Medora's mother had given a logger a ride across and, on the return trip, a cable let go, catapulting her into the frigid water.

Medora's younger brothers and sisters came running back to the cookhouse, saying Mother had fallen into the river. They thought Mother was gone for good.

The men took another bateau out to the site of the accident. They found Medora's mother with her hands frozen to the gunwales. Happily, she had popped up right beside the boat and grabbed hold.

They took her to the cookhouse, set her by the woodstove, and thawed her out.

batt'ry
Battery

A visitor from the Midwest parks his car on Main Street and walks down the sidewalk. He hadn't gotten far when a local says, "You got a good batt'ry?" The Midwesterner, thinking the man wants a jumpstart, says he does indeed have a good battery, and if the fellow needs assistance getting his car going, he'd be delighted to accommodate.

"How can I help you?" asks the Midwesterner with a warm Midwestern grin. "Don't need help," the local says. "You left your headlights on."

bawn
Given birth to

If you were bawn in New Hampshire, you might be a native.

baysta
A large specimen

"Did you get your deah this ye-ah?"
"I guess. Eight-point buck. A baysta."

bayuh

1. A large animal that hibernates in the winter

Our bayuhs are black. A black bayuh in the wild has never killed a person in New Hampshire. Yet. But a black bayuh could do a job on you if he wanted.

Newcomers to Bethlehem had been told to watch out or the bayuhs would get after their garbage. To be safe, they locked four bags of garbage in the cab of the truck to be taken to the dump the next day. So the bags wouldn't smell up the truck too bad, they left the window open a crack. This was their mistake. The bayuh smelled the garbage, smashed the window, and absconded with three of the bags.

"Could have been worse," the newcomers said. "At least we had just one bag to take to the dump."

2. Unadorned, nude

I got a call from Ada. She and her husband, Urban, have a camp across the lake from ours. "Get in your kayak and paddle down here quick if you want to see a bayuh," she said.

I did. I got in the kayak and paddled across the lake and down the shore toward their place. As I got closer I saw Pudgy and Joe on Joe's beach. They were sitting in lawn chairs and looking in the direction of Ada and Urban's camp. I squinted and could see Urban on the far side of the picnic table with a camera, and, yes, the black shape of a bayuh halfway up the trunk of the big pine tree.

A couple of other boats had anchored near Ada and Urban's dock. They were watching the bayuh, too.

I paddled faster, wanting to get a good look at that bayuh before he ran off. I could hear Joe yelling something. As I paddled in closer, I finally understood. Joe was yelling, "Urban, go in the house and put some pants on!"

Urban had been taking a nap when Ada spotted the bayuh. He got so excited, he jumped out of bed and ran out in the yard, practically bayuh.

BBs in a boxcar

Small objects in a large space

"If that fella had any brains at all, they'd roll around in his skull like BBs in a boxcar."

be-ah

Alcoholic beverage made with hops and best consumed cold

This particular lady moved into town. Right off she spotted Skip on the side of the road, having a be-ah. She reported him to the police, said he was breaking the open-container law.

The chief gave Skip a call and they had a chat.

Skip said nothing to the particular lady. He waited a while. Then one evening, after dark, he parked his truck out front of her house.

And left it there 'til morning.

beats nawthin'

Better than nothing at all

"Sorry, Fred, it's beans for breakfast, agin."

"Beats nawthin'."

beauty

1. Something or someone pleasant to look at

"Miss New Hampshire, now she's a real beauty."

2. The opposite of beauty; something or someone unpleasant or unworthy

"That fella sold me the van with the gimpy transmission; he's a beauty."

"You ain't just a-kiddin'. I dropped off a lawn mower at the dump last fall. Wunt cut for beans. The little weasel picked it up, painted it red, cleaned up the spark plug, replaced a couple hoses, and sold it to me for seventy-five bucks. Still wunt cut for beans."

"Don't you just hate it when you buy back your own junk?"

"It's ignominious."

"Don't know about that, but it's kind of embarrassing."

beeswax

Personal business or concern

"How's that hemorrhoid? Shrunk yet?"

"None of your beeswax, Pa."

Also: Mind your own beeswax.

"You and Molly going to the movies Saddy night?"

"Mind your own beeswax, Ma."

bettah b'lieve it

It's true!

At the paper mill some of the workers kept fishing gear in their lockers and on break would fish off the dam. Rene caught three big fish.

Normand said, "You're not going to eat those, are you, Rene?" (The river was heavily polluted.)

"I'll give one to my mother-in-law. If she don't die, I'll eat the other two."

On Monday, Normand said, "Rene, I saw your mother-in-law at church."

Rene said, "Them fish were good! Bettah b'lieve it."

bettah than a poke in the eye with a shahp stick

Most things are

"How'd that open-heart surgery go, Leland?"

"Bettah than a poke in the eye with a shahp stick."

biddy

1. An old bird

Several of Hap's biddies came up missing from the chicken house. He said to his thieving neighbor: "Be sure not to let your chickens out. They might come home."

2. An old woman with a fowl attitude

Barbara at Colebrook Commons Senior Center told about her grandfather Josiah Piper, a dyed-in-the-wool Yankee who always wore a union suit to bed until he married the schoolmarm, who was kinda tony and a bit of an old biddy. She insisted Josiah wear a nightshirt. Those nightshirts weren't all that big and didn't give the coverage a union suit did, but Josiah succumbed.

In the middle of the night, a commotion erupted in the henhouse.

Josiah jumped out of bed, loaded his firing piece, and ran to the coop. He poked his shotgun through the little door and bent low to see inside.

Just then Old Spot, the hound dog, came up behind Josiah and put his cold nose where the sun don't shine. Startled, Josiah pulled the trigger and killed fifteen chickens.

big-ass

Larger than most of its kind; usually, but not always, applied to vehicles

A Hummer (pronounced *Humma*) is a big-ass car. Melanie drives a big-ass Harley with a sidecar for her big-ass dog.

John launched his big-ass boat on a hafassed pond, irritating the locals and the pickerel.

Bigfoot

New Hampshire's version of Sasquatch

Our Bigfoots are not quite as big as the Northwestern variety. Then again, we are a small state. Though they try to keep a low profile, Bigfoots are spotted out and about fairly often, usually during deer-hunting season, when more people are in the woods. The thing is, being reserved and somewhat taciturn, we don't talk much about Bigfoot sightings. Besides, people might think we were nuts. Occasionally, the subject comes up in conversation.

"I seen what I seen," the hunter confided.

"You didn't see a Bigfoot. I don't b'lieve it."

"I did. It stood under an apple tree, reached up ten feet, and grabbed a McIntosh off a branch."

"If there's Bigfoots in New Hampshire, then how did they get here?"

"UFOs brung 'em."

birda

A person whose hobby is spotting birds in the wild and learning their names

Birdas often go into the swamps or mountains looking for birds they've never seen before. They hang binoculars around their necks and write down the names of the birds, as well as the date and location of the sighting. New Hampshire is loaded with birds, and not just at the State House in January.

Even folks who are not hahd-coah birdas get curious when they see birds they don't recognize. A woman from the city, new to Hollis, called a birda and described a large brown bird fluttering and pecking by her stone wall.

The birda said it was probably a turkey.

"No," the woman said. "This has feathers."

22

biscuits

A Yankee diet staple made from flour, cream of tartar, and shortening

We eat our biscuits with buttah, maple syrup, or rhubarb sauce. We use them in our favorite strawberry shortcake. We call it strawberry shortcake even though there's no cake, just biscuits, strawberries, and whipped cream.

In Chatham, locals reminisced about snowmobiling on rough trails where the bumps, struck at a good clip, would send you flying.

One guy says, "I hit a big mogul so hahd, Muhtha almost flew off the back of the snow machine. Glad she didn't. She makes awful good biscuits."

blackfly season

Generally runs from Muhtha's Day to Fatha's Day

Gardeners wear nets head to toe for protection, because bug dope does not deter blackflies, although some swear by Avon Skin So Soft.

Early in the season, bites are apt to swole up, but after the first 15 or 20, your body adjusts and hardly swoles at all. A swarm of blackflies will drive a lumberjack or a moose to his knees.

When they get real bad, we say, "The blackflies are wicked."

When they get even thicker, we say, "The blackflies are solid."

Best to stay inside when the blackflies are solid.

Old saying: Thank God for blackflies. Otherwise, everybody'd want to live in New Hampshire.

black ice

Extra-slippery ice

When black ice forms on the road, stay home. You can't see it because it's the same color as the tar, and if you hit a patch, even if you're going real slow, you're apt to slide off into the ditch. New Hampshirites aren't daunted by much in the way of driving conditions, but we steer clear of black ice.

blinka

Turn signal

Mac got stopped for failing to use his blinka when he turned onto his road. "Your turn signal appears to be defective," the police officer said.

"It ain't," Mac said. "Dint need it. Everybody knows where I live."

bloodsuckah

Leech

If you wade in mucky ponds, you might find a few bloodsuckahs attached to your calves when you go to put your sneakers back on. Trout eat bloodsuckahs, but no one else seems to enjoy them much. If you cut the head off a nightwalker and thread it on your hook, sometimes a trout with a low IQ will think it's a bloodsuckah and bite it.

bo-ahd

1. Plank; a strip of lumber like a two-by-four

A fella from away suggested this as the quintessential sentence for demonstrating the New Hampshire accent: "If you leave them bo-ahds in the doah yahd and it rains, they'll wop." He actually heard his next-door neighbor say that, and it took him several days to translate it: "If you leave the boards in the door yard and it rains, they'll warp."

2. Filled with ennui

An eight-year-old at the opera might get bo-ahd after an hour or two. (And so mightn't I.)

bobba

A red-and-white plastic globe clipped on to monofilament fish line

Bobbas float on top of the water. When a fish takes your bait, the bobba bobs under, so you know you've got a bite. The bobbin' motion of the bobba is your cue to set the hook and reel in.

Because I like to fish, my friend Neil English, who's handy, made me a set of bobba earrings. They're real pretty and elicit a lot of comments when I wear them out. One time our friend Maren, who's from Iowa and has lived in New England only a few decades, couldn't understand what Neil and I were talking about when the discussion turned to bobbas. We explained. Evidently they don't use bobbas in Iowa. Don't know as they even have lakes.

Later, Neil decorated a pine tree all over with bobbas, and we dropped it off on Maren's lawn as a Christmas surprise.

bob house
A portable shack for fishing through the ice

Instead of bobbin' for apples, you bob for lake trout or pickerel. Anglers use jiggas for jiggin'. They sit on a stool (or recliner) by the hole, and move the wooden jigga up and down in a scientific way. The lake trout, way down deep, notice the shiner on the end of the line, jiggin' around, and, if they're in the mood, bite it.

On big lakes in midwinter, bob house villages pop up, only to disappear before ice-out. Fella from away, driving by Winnisquam in February, noticed the shacks on the ice. He said to his companion: "I realized money was tight up here, but that's ridiculous." He thought he was looking at a shantytown. On the contrary, some deluxe bob houses come equipped with stoves, lights, bookshelves, televisions, easy chairs, toilets, W-iFi, Jacuzzis, and bars. I saw this ad in *The Concord Monitor*: "Bob house for sale. 7' x 12'. Sleeps 4."

Of course, the truly hearty eschew bob houses. They fish in the open air, sometimes building a small fire on shore, augering out a bunch of holes, and watching eagle-eyed for the flags on the tip-ups to tip up. They might cook a hot dog over a campfire or consume a beer or two while waiting. When a pickerel grabs the bait, the taut line flips a lever, and the flag pops up. Then the fisherman runs like hell across the ice to set the hook and pull the pickerel in, should the pickerel decide to stick around that long.

Now, that's entertaining—watching those fishermen in their snowsuits and heavy boots scamper out across the pond.

bog

A muddy, watery place, sometimes called a meadow; not so fancy as a wetland nor as extensive as a swamp

If you try to slog through a bog to cut some cat-o-nine tails or pussy willows, you might get bogged down. Blood suckahs enjoy a good bog.

boiled dinner

A New England specialty of corned beef or pork shoulder simmered for hours with potatoes, beets, onions, carrots, and turnips. Some tasty!

Next day, chop and fry the leftovers as red-flannel hash and use the broth as a base for pea soup. Not exactly hotty quizeen but delicious, nutritious, and filling.

bones

A traditional handheld percussion instrument similar to spoons

Betty Gordon felt sad that her friend, musician Cecil Rivers, died on his way home from a Christmas concert. "But," she said, "he left his bones to me."

boneyahd

Cemetery, graveyard

At the Women's Club meeting held in the Presbyterian Church in Bedford, I asked who among the members was a native of Bedford. Not one hand went up.

"Where are the natives?" I said, appalled.

After a pause, one woman pointed at the big windows. We all looked at the boneyahd on the hill.

The Canterbury Shakers, a religious sect known for celibacy, ingenuity, and efficiency, took out all the stones in their boneyahd to use for walls and foundations. They replaced the individual stones with one big one. Why? Easier mowing.

Boston Post cane

In 1909, the Boston Post *newspaper donated 431 inscribed, gold-headed walking sticks to 431 New England towns. Officials were to seek out the oldest man in town and present him with the cane. In 1930, the rules changed and women became eligible, so the cane went to the oldest person. When that person died, the cane passed to the next in line.*

Some people were none too pleased to receive the cane. Some called it "the death cane," and refused it outright.

One evening at a speaking engagement in Salisbury I asked if there were any natives in the crowd. Several people pointed to a woman in the front row. I asked, "You're a native?"

"No," she said. "I moved here when I was five years old. But I am the oldest person in town. The holder of the *Boston Post* cane."

"Oh," I said, "isn't that wonderful? How old are you?"

She said, "None of your damn business."

'bout froze

Experience a chilling cold

"They had the air conditioner cranked so high I 'bout froze. If you ask me, ninety-nine percent of the time, air conditioners are like the city of Boston."

"How's that?"

"Unnecessary."

bowteek

A shop that sells clothes and accessories for small people with big money

bring your pocketbook

A warning that an event, activity, or purchase will be expensive

"That bowteek on Washington Street has a lot of pretty things, but bring your pocketbook."

broke out

Released

Harriet says to the neighbor who shoveled the end of her driveway, "Thanks for getting me broke out. My snowblower's broke or I woulda done it myself. I'd buy a new one down to the Home Depot, except I'm broke."

brought up in a bahn

If someone leaves a door open, the housekeeper might comment:"What were you, brought up in a bahn?"

Most days, farmers leave the bahn door open so the chickens and cows can go in and out as they please.

Related term: Your bahn door is open. Meaning the fly on a man's trousers is down.

browned up

Dark; slightly burnt

Some like their toast light and soft. I like it crunchy and browned up with a sprinkling of sugar on the char.

bruhtha

Sista's male sibling

brung

Past tense of bring

"Did you bring the mushmellows for s'mores?"
"I brung 'em."

bubluh

A fountain for drinking at school, in an office building, park, or public building

You don't need a cup, much less a plastic bottle, to enjoy refreshment from a bubluh. And the water's local, not imported from Fiji or Maine.

bug dope

Mosquito repellent

At town meeting, debate raged over a warrant article to raise and appropriate $2,000 to have the village sprayed against mosquitoes. Some worried about the health risks of the chemicals. Others, like Catherine, just couldn't stand another mosquito infestation.

Catherine said: "I was holding a cookout and the mosquitoes were so thick we had to move everything inside. I couldn't even enjoy the outdoors around my home. It was terrible!"

Vin spoke up. "Mr. Moderator, I'd like to propose an amendment. Amend down from two thousand to a dollah ninety-eight. Buy Catherine a can of bug dope."

bum

1. In England, it's your backside or rear end

2. In the city, it's a politically incorrect name for a homeless person

3. A bum knee pains you

4. In a bum deal, you get the short end of the stick—that is, shafted.

In Chocorua they tell about summer resident William James, brother to the famous writer Henry James. A Harvard man and great intellect, William was determined to master the art of Yankee trading. Off he went looking for a horse. He found one for sale. "How much do you want for that horse?" William James asked the trader.

"How much do you have?"

"A hundred-fifty dollars."

"Well," says the trader, "that's the price."

William James returned with the horse, some proud of his negotiating, but most folks thought he talked himself into a bum deal.

bump

A frost heave of mammoth proportions, or a big hole in the road

Driving a five-mile stretch of dug-up road under construction at about five miles per hour, I noticed the drivers coming in the other direction looked like bobbleheads, the road was so rough. At the end of the ordeal, just before corduroy turned to tar, was a single sign: BUMP. (See Yankee humor.)

bunged up

Hurt, but not as badly as if you were stove up

"When Ted tripped over Maryanne's Saint Bernard, he got bunged up."

burn off

Evaporate under the hot sun

Summer doesn't last long in New Hampshire, but at least it's better than in Maine, where they consider themselves lucky if summer comes on a weekend and stays until Monday. In New

Hampshire, we expect, and usually get, at least a week or two of hot weather, requiring (for the spleeny) air-conditioning in upstairs bedrooms for a night or two. If a day starts out hazy, we say, "Maybe it'll burn off," meaning maybe by 10 or 11 o'clock, the sun will be shining. And often it is!

buttah

Made from cow milk churned until it's solid

The city boy sat on the milking stool ready to milk his first cow. He looked the belly and udders all over, then, confused, asked the farmer, "How do you turn it on?"

The farmer said, "Pull her tail."

button up

Get ready

Come fall we button up for winter. This means putting on the storm windows if you have them, or covering windows and all but one door with plastic as a barrier against the cold. Also, laying tubes of fabric filled with sand on windowsills and doorsills to block the draft. And banking pine boughs around the foundation, as well as piling the wood in a convenient location. Make sure the chimbley's clean and the furnace tuned. Oil tank full. Fall is our busy season.

"You all buttoned up for winter, Everett?"

"Bring 'er on."

Butt-ugly

Especially unattractive

Usually applied to objects, not people. "It's a reliable old truck but butt-ugly. Looks like somebody gave it a paint job with a mop."

buzz

Call on the telephone

"Give me a buzz if you want to go to the beach after it burns off."

In the days of party lines (more than one family on the same phone line), people would give other people buzzes and sometimes, shockingly, neighbors would listen in.

Hattie from Hebron was infamous for listening in on other people's conversations. One time a couple of her neighbors were talking on the phone when they happened to think that maybe Hattie was eavesdropping. So one yelled into the receiver: "Hattie, hang up the phone!"

Hattie yelled back: "I ain't listening. I'm clear over by the sink."

by side

Beside or at the side of

"Muhtha, stack that cod of wood by side the shed."

C

cabbige

Structure spanning a river

It might sound like the main ingredient in coleslaw, but if a new kid asks a native kid in Andover where the best fishing spot is, the native kid is apt to say: "Stand on the cabbige."

This happened to one young fellow, who subsequently asked his dad, "Where are the cabbages along the river?"

"The cabbages?"

It was a puzzlement, until father and son took their poles to the river and found the natives fishing off the bridge—the one for cars as opposed to trains. That's right, the car bridge, which, in the vernacular and spoken fast comes out cabbige.

cah

Automobile

At the annual meeting of the New Hampshire Model T Club, I heard the story of Mark Winkley's cah. He owned a beauty of Model T, but it burned up in a barn fire. The other club members donated spare parts and, with a bit of tinkering, Mark had another Model T to drive. And drive it he did, all over the state. You never knew where Mark would show up on a fine day—down to Keene, up to Conway, over to Orford.

His son said, "Dad, you'll have that cah all wore out by the time I inherit it. Won't you try to keep the mileage down?"

Mark said, "I think I'm going to be buried in this cah."

"Why's that?"

"I never saw a hole a Model T couldn't get out of."

cahd

Humorous or eccentric person

Estalyn was a cahd from Greenfield. When I asked for stories from the audience, she said, "I've got a story to tell, but before I do, you should know I'm ninety-eight years old and my story might be a little off-color."

I said, "Estalyn, you go right ahead and tell it."

And she did.

And it was.

And they're still talking about it in Greenfield.

cahkiss

1. Dead body

Ann came up against this word when she moved to Amherst. She'd never used a dump before—always had her garbage picked up in the city where she came from. Wanting to do the right thing, she visited town hall where she found the chief of police. She told him she wished to dispose of her rubbish properly and asked about dump regulations.

He thought a minute, then said: "No hoss monooah or dead cahkisses."

She thanked him, though she said, "I had no idea what he was talking about."

She needn't have worried. Turns out she didn't own a horse nor did she have any corpses she needed to get rid of.

2. Live body, but a tired one

Sometimes a living person can feel like a cahkiss, as in, "I was so tired from running that marathon it was all I could do to haul my cahkiss up the stayahs to bed."

camp

A cabin or small house used as a getaway; might be on a lake or a river or deep in the woods

Hunting camps are used as bases for hunting expeditions. And socializing. And drinking. Fishing camps, same thing.

A cabin can be a camp, but it could also be a house. A trailer can also be a camp. If it's modest and used seasonally, it's a camp.

A logging camp is a makeshift set of buildings and equipment on a logging site.

A sleepaway camp houses children whose parents want to get rid of them for the summer. Usually on a lake. At sleepaway camps, children make jewelry out of twine, learn to shoot with bows and arrows, canoe, swim, and sing silly songs. These camps often have strange names like Wanagohom.

cannery

A yellow bird

Leo says, "I bought my wife a cannery for her birthday. Boy, can that cannery sing."

cant dog

Logging tool

A highly valued logging tool used to persuade logs to move downriver, a cant dog is an iron hook with two prongs, one straight, one curved, on a sturdy wooden handle.

In logging camps, only half in jest, they said if the river driver fell in, "Save the cant dog and to heck with the man."

capet

Floor covering, a big rug; Aladdin rode around on a magic one.

In spring, a good housekeeper hangs the capet on the clothesline and uses a capet beater to beat out winter's dirt.

Another cleaning method: Snowing a capet. I've done it myself. You throw a capet out onto the fresh snow facedown. Then turn it and sweep vigorously. You'd be surprised how much dirt peels off.

cat ice

Ice so thin only a cat could walk across it and not fall through

cellah

In some parts of the country, houses have basements dug into the ground. Here we have cellahs.

When we descend the steps to get a jar of tomatoes, we go down cellah. If we go down cellah to get into the hard cider, we go down much faster than we go up.

cellah hole

When the house is long gone, the cellah hole remains along with the foundation stones, typically granite.

A joke among firefighters: "We save a lot of cellah holes."

Century Club

Group of crazy people

People who have walked the perimeter of the Mount Washington Observatory's deck when the wind was blowing 100 miles per hour or more belong to the Century Club.

To become a member, you must walk the whole way around without being knocked down or touching your hands to the floor. (Thanks to Eric Pinder for the scoop on this elite group.)

chahm

1. Something that brings you luck

2. When something works like a chahm, it works well

3. A chahmin' person is pleasant to be around

Also chahmah: "The neighbor put up a eight-foot fence, plastered it with NO TRESPASSING signs, and said if he caught the kids stepping foot on his property again he'd pepper them with bird shot. What a chahmah."

chimbley

Chimney

"I swiped the bricks from that falling-down chimbley by the old cellah hole and laid 'em in Althea's gahdin for a walkway. Wa'n't she tickled."

Chippa Granite

A rosy-cheeked cartoon boy who symbolized the wholesome goodness of our homegrown farm products; he was featured on posters and brochures promoting milk, vegetables, and fruits in the 1950s.

chippa shredda

A useful piece of equipment that can reduce a brush pile to mulch in hardly any time at all. Can be dangerous if not used with care.

One year for my birthday, my husband gave me a home-printed gift certificate for a chippa shredda. Never got the chippa shredda, but it was fun imagining what it would be like to own one. Maybe he (or I) was too cheap to fork over the money. Or maybe somebody warned John not to follow through on the gift certificate: "You give Beck a chippa shredda, and the next thing you know, she'll be squirting out the other end." (See "nimrod.")

chittah

The sound a squirrel makes

Alden Farrar of Warner tells this story. "My ancestor that I was named for went out hunting and there on a high branch was a squirrel, just chittahrin' away. So old Alden loaded up his muzzle-loader, and I guess he overloaded it, because when he went to shoot at the squirrel, which was still up there chittahrin', the muzzleloader bucked and knocked him ass over teakettle. When Alden come to his senses, stretched out on the ground, muzzle-loader still in hand, the squirrel was still chittahrin' on that high branch. Old Alden said: 'Chittah, damn you, chittah! You wouldn't be chittahrin' if you were on the other end of this thing.' "

chuckaberry

This red berry grows close to the ground, one or two to a plant. The leaves are dark green and the berries taste minty; also called pahtridge berries.

My grown daughter and I were walking in the woods. She picked a berry and said, "Mom, what do you call this?"

I said, "Chuckaberry."

She said, "How do you spell it?"

I said, "C-H-E-C-K-E-R-B-E-R-R-Y."

chuck it

Throw it away

"You want the rest of my bread puddin'?"

"Gross. Chuck it."

To upchuck is to chuck from within.

cider apples

Bruised, wormy, and/or drops; those that fell to the ground before anybody could pluck them from the tree

Not good for eating, pies, or even sauce, but good enough to press into cider.

clairbuds or clahbids

The horizontal wooden siding on a home, sometimes spelled "clapboard"

We like to let various coverings age on our outside walls. Start with tarpaper. Let that set a year or two. Move on to Tyvek. Leave that up for a spell. Then, when you're ready, apply clairbuds. No rush, because once you get the place completely clairbudded, your property taxes will go up. If you paint the clairbuds, your taxes will go up even more.

clannish

Sticking with one's own kind

At the mill, two men ran for the office of shop steward. In this branch of the union there were 98 Frenchmen and 2 Norwegians. When the ballots were counted, it was 98 for Pierre and 2 for Lars. Maurice says to Louis, "Those Norwegians, damn clannish, ain't they?"

clip

When you move fast, you're going at a good clip, or clippin' right along.

Probably has to do with those fast-moving clipper ships that sailed the high seas.

Edith at 90 years old was still driving and known around town as a terror on the road. Her friend Helen caught a ride with her one day. As they approached a yield sign, Edith was going along at a good clip, Helen spotted a car to the left, also approaching the intersection, also at a good clip. Edith didn't slow down. Instead of yielding, she kept a-going. "Edith," Helen yelled, "yield!"

"No," Edith said. "I yielded last time!"

closnuf

Almost perfect

"This shelf hanging straight?"

"Closnuf."

Often used in the phrase, "Closnuf for government work," meaning, "We did our best and that'll just have to be goodnuf."

cock

1. Prounounced cawk, *a rooster*

2. A bottle plug

Sometimes when you open champagne, it pops its cock. Similarly, when a person gets angry and says something maybe he shouldn't, he popped his cock.

3. The sealer used to keep windowpanes in place, or the cracks around bathtubs from leaking

You apply cock with a cockin' gun.

cockah

Something especially nice

"That new four-wheeler of yours is a cockah."

"Bought it off Rodger for fifty bucks. Cleaned it up, sprayed some quick staht in the carburetor, put a dose of dragass in the tank, runs slick as a bean."

Variation: cockin', as in "That pee-not no-ah (Pinot Noir) wine is cockin' good."

cocked

Inebriated

"Wesley, if you go hawnpouting in that tippy boat and get cocked, you'll end up in the drink."

cod

1. A delicious white-fleshed saltwater fish, great for chowdah

2. Measurement for wood, spelled "cord" but pronounced cod. It's four feet by four feet by eight feet of stacked stove wood.

"Come January, when the electric goes out and the furnace chokes up, that cod wood sure comes in handy."

3. What you use to plug an appliance in to an electric outlet.

"The cod on the toastah was worn through to the wire. When Doug plugged it in, sparks flew, and he got electrifried."
"Is he okay?"
"Just singed. But the toastah's deader'n a doahnail."

coffin

1. A casket for burying the dead

Mother was a little hard to get along with, so when she died, the family had mixed feelings. They laid her out in the coffin in the living room and the boys loaded the coffin onto a sledge for transport to the cemetery. Unfortunately, the sledge got away from them, slid fast down the hill, and banged into a big pine tree at the bottom. The coffin popped open and Mother sat up. Alive and sputtering.

She lived another fifteen years, even harder to get along with than before. Well, death comes to us all, and once again it came for Mother. They loaded her into the coffin, loaded the coffin onto the sledge, and started out for the cemetery. At the top of the hill, Father cautioned: "Hold tight, boys, and mind that big pine tree."

2. Expectorating

"You keep coffin' like that, you'll go into cardiac arrest and end up in a coffin."

Old saying: "It was not the cough that carried him off, it was the coffin they carried him off in."

41

Cog, the
Also known as the railway to the moon, which is an exaggeration

When the Cog Railway's builder Sylvester Marsh asked permission to build a railroad to the top of Mount Washington, the legislators down to Concord thought his idea was so outlandish, they said: "Go ahead and build a railway to the moon for all we care." The Cog doesn't go all the way to the moon, but it does climb the highest mountain in the northeastern United States, and has done since its maiden chug on July 3, 1869.

colder than a well-digger's ass
Uncomfortably chilly; cold as a witch's tit, but damp, too

cold snap
A period of sudden, extreme cold

"That was some cold snap. The hands on the town clock froze."

come-along
Winch

David said: "We use the come-along to drag the boat out of the lake when it sinks, which it does every fall come the big rains. We named it the Jacques Cousteau, because it spends so much time underwater."

comical
Funny

"His feet went right out from under him and he rolled down the snowbank and landed in a heap. If he'd got hurt it wouldn't have been comical, but he dint, so it was."

comical bugga (also comical jigga)

Funny person

Kendall Morse, Maine storyteller, he's a comical bugga.

Adam Sandler is a comical jigga. He's from New Hampshire. Also Sarah Silverman and Tom Bergeron—two other comical Granite State jiggas.

common

1. A village green

"The gazebo on the common looks pretty, all lit up with those strings of white lights."

2. Regular, or in the normal way

"She was just walking along the road common when her knee let go and down she went."

con

1. As a verb, to trick someone

2. As a noun, tasty ears that grow on stalks; some varieties can be popped.

I grew up on Con Hill Road (spelled Corn Hill Road) in Boscawen. They used to grow a lot of con on Con Hill Road. Not so much anymore. It's all built up.

At the Wolfeboro farmstand the customer says, "Is this con picked fresh?"

"No. We picked it stale this mornin'."

concubine

A wide cloth girdle for men

Hazel said, "It was a beautiful wedding. The bride had a ten-foot train and her gown was covered with beadin'. The groom and groomsmen all wore white tuxedos with concubines around their waists."

copascetic

Harmonious; A-OK

> "Carol and Mel still feuding?"
> "Nope. Everything's copascetic."

cottage

A mansion in the mountains

Rich folks who built big, beautiful homes on the slopes of the White Mountains during the late 1800s and early 1900s called them cottages, evidently to discourage relations from visiting.

Less-expensive homes were called summer places.

coulda been worse

Yankee mantra

Almost anything coulda been worse, if you think about it. Also the title of my fifth book, except I called it *Could Have Been Worse*, as a concession to readers from away.

In Randolph, they tell the harrowing story of the lumberjack who felled a tree the wrong way and got his arm pinned. To save his life—knowing that help might never come—he sawed off his arm. Then he had to walk a mile out of the woods to his truck, carrying the severed limb. After that, he had to drive himself, one-armed, to the hospital, where they reattached it.

Pretty bad. But as the lumberjack said, "Coulda been worse. Coulda been my head."

In Newmarket the scaffolding on the house collapsed and William got a pile of bricks on his head. "Coulda been worse," his buddy said. "At least he had group insurance."

couplethree
Two or three

"Andy's been working for the bridge crew for a couplethree weeks. Let's hope he can hold on to this job longer than the last one."

covered bridge
A bridge with a roof

New Hampshire has many, including ones in Andover, Swanzey, Hopkinton, Cornish, Plainfield, Newport, Bath, Lyme, Stark, Bartlett, and Jackson. And that's just for starters.

A traveler from New Jersey asked directions at a roadside stand. The proprietor gave detailed directions, which the traveler repeated step by step. "And then," the traveler said, "I go over the covered bridge."

"If I were you," the proprietor said, "I'd go through it."

cow pie
What comes out of the south end of a cow; also cow flap, cow flop, and cow putty

Some nonprofit organizations hold cow-pie bingo contests as fund-raisers. A field is divided up like a big checkerboard, and participants buy tickets for squares. Then the cow is set loose. The holder of the ticket corresponding to the first square to be blessed with a cow pie wins the prize. It's quite an event to watch. Sometimes the cow holds back for hours, as spectators' tensions mount. This tradition is believed to have originated in Vermont.

cowt
Beware

"Cowt, Herb, there's a seagull directly overhead and she looks loaded for bayuh."

Or, "The driveway's a skating ring. Cowt. You don't want to do a cowt-ow and fall on your can."

Cowt-ow is, of course, a related term, meaning slip and fall like an ice skater failing to land a jump. In a classic cowt-ow, somebody yells, "Cowt, Scotty," and Scotty yells, "Ow" as he does a cowt-ow and lands hard.

crackadon
Morning

Elsie's mother put her to bed with the admonition: "I don't want you to get up before the crackadon."

Elsie listened all night, but she never heard it.

crazier than a rat in a coffee can
Lacking even a modicum of common sense

"Derek traded his Toyota for a thirdhand Cadillac. He always was crazier than a rat in a coffee can when it come to big vehicles with big engines."

creeahsoot
Clogs your chimbley when you burn green wood

In some quatuhs, a chimbley fire is considered nature's way of clearing out the creeahsoot. Which is fine, as long as the timbers don't catch, or the shingles, and as long as the blocks don't crack.

One night some friends and I were driving through Nottingham on 152. We spotted flames shooting about ten feet out the top of a center chimbley. Feeling heroic, we pulled into the driveway, ran up to the door, and knocked frantically. A man in long johns cracked the door about a quatuh the way.

"You've got a chimbley fie-uh!" we said.

"So," he said.

cripe or cripes

An expression of surprise

"You ordering the tripe, Mike? Cripe. I didn't think you'd go in for that sort of thing. Had you pegged as a grilled-cheese guy."

"Was that the road I was supposed to take? Cripes, I'm goin' to have to pull a U-ee."

cross

Displeased, angry

Lydia was helping her husband Floyd with the haying when she reached into the wrong place on the machine and her hand got pinched bad. Her fingers were all bent and the hand started to swole. "I'm going back to the house and soak it," she said.

Floyd was cross. "Who's gonna help with the haying now?"

cross-threaded

Stuck in deep ruts

Charter Weeks offered this example: "If you go down Scruton Pond Road, be careful you don't get cross-threaded or you'll end up all the way to 202 before you can turn around."

Relationships can also be cross-threaded.

On the wagon ride home from the cemetery where he'd just buried his wife, Cyrus got to ruminating with his old friend Jeremiah: "Jerry," he said, "my wife was a wonderful mother to my seven children. She was a wonderful cook, too. Her biscuits would melt in your mouth. Big in the church, always helping out at the socials and so forth. And what a worker! She could work all day in the field and hahdly break a sweat."

"She were a wonder," Jerry said.

"You know, Jerry," Cyrus said. "I never really liked her."

47

crusha

A hoppa with hydraulics at the dump that compacts refuse for disposal

A selectman, in a town I won't name, showed up at the dump kinda unsteady on his feet. Maybe it was mouthwash that made his breath so tangy. Maybe not. Anyway, this selectman was heaving a kind of a heavy bag into the crusha. He swung it back and forth like a pendulum, and as he worked up to the big swing to toss it, evidently he forgot to let go. He and the bag both sailed over the railing. Down they went.

Luckily, the dump master saw the selectman's predicament and hit the shutoff. He stepped out of his little dump-master cottage, strode up to the crusha with hands on hips. "Get outta there," he said. "Selectmen don't belong in the crusha. They belong over in compost."

cuff

Slap

"There's a white-tailed hawnet buzzing around my head, but I don't dare cuff it. If I cuff it, it'll get ugly and sting me."

cunnin'

Cute and adorable

Infants are cunnin', except for the homely ones. That is, the ones that aren't related to you.

Can also refer to the charming, unselfconscious actions of the very young. Frannie said, "In kindygahden, the kids were playing with big plastic screws, nuts, and gears, building pretend machines. Wally comes home one day. He says, 'Grammie, I'm the best screwer in my class.' Wa'n't that cunnin'?"

cuss-ed

Darned

"That cuss-ed television blew up in the middle of the Celtics game."

D

dahkuh than a stack of black cats

As the housemate of a black cat named Rosie, I can attest that a stack of black cats must indeed be very dahk.

dahnin' needle

Dragonfly

When I was a kid out in the boat still-fishing, dahnin' needles would land on the gunnels or the rods or on us. My mother said if I swore, the dahnin' needle would sew my mouth closed. So I didn't.

A story from Judy Whitcomb: Brother said a bad word. Mother said, "We don't talk like that at home. Pack your bags."

So the little guy packed his bags.

His littler sister said, 'Brotha, where you gonna sleep?"

"How the hell do I know?"

da-ow

No; not really

Vic visited his neighbor's farm and found Moe feeding his sow, Chops, from a slop bucket with a teaspoon. "Don't it take a ridiculous amount of time to feed a pig with a teaspoon?" Vic said.

"Da-ow," Moe said. "Time don't mean nothin' to a pig."

dead cahkiss

Extra-ripe corpse

This is an awful story, but true. One winter, the family cat died. The ground was too frozen to bury it, so Dad put the deceased in a garbage bag and stuck it in a hauling trailer around the side of the house. Forgot about it.

Come Easter, Mom hid Merle's basket full of goodies in the crotch of the maple tree.

49

"Didn't the bunny come, Mommy?" little Merle asked.

"You'll have to look and see."

Merle looked and looked. He found the garbage bag in the hauling trailer, opened it up, and found the dead cahkiss inside. He came in crying: "That's not a very good present!"

deader'n a doornail

No signs of vitality

"Tractor wunt staht. Batt'ry's deader'n a doornail."

deader'n Maynard Record's beagle dog

Long dead; truly dead (coined by David Emerson)

Maynard Record's beagle liked to lie in the middle of the crossroads serving the sister cities of Chatham, N.H., and Stow, Maine, where David grew up. Folks knew to drive around the dog even in thick fog or snowstorms.

Years passed. The dog died. But so ingrained was the habit of driving around Maynard Record's beagle dog, the locals still swerve.

deaf as a haddock

Unable to hear

"When the dog gets his nose on a scent, he goes deaf as a haddock. I can yell all day, but he just ignores me."

"Did he come from Maine?"

"He did. How did you know?"

"My wife's from Maine."

deah

1. A term of affection

Some of us never use "deah" as a term of affection. For many Yankees, the closest we get to a term of affection is "you," as in "How are you?" or "What you up to?" or "Haven't seen you around lately." The ones who do say deah say it so often, they make up for the rest of us.

Years ago Eunice waitressed at a fancy resort in the White Mountains, where rich folks came to stay all summer. One guest, a little old lady, was among her charges for breakfast, dinnah, and suppah every day. This guest never ordered anything off the menu. Every meal had special instructions and required a lot of attention.

After about three weeks, the little old lady slipped Eunice a 50-cent piece at suppah and whispered: "You can expect this every month, deah."

2. An antlered animal prized by hunters

"Deah, did you get your deah this yeah?"
"None of us got our deah this yeah, deah. Except Ma."
"What'd she get it with?"
"The Buick."

deah season
Time of year when you can hunt deah

Pay close attention to the rules and regulations. They're complicated and vary county to county. Sometimes you can hunt with bow and arrow, or muzzleloader, or rifle. Sometimes you're allowed to shoot the ones with antlers, but not the bald-headed ones. It's a scientific culling of the herd. If you make a mistake, you might get pinched.

The new minister in Epsom was driving along North Road in the evening when he spotted a beautiful animal standing in the field, a deah. He shined his lights on the animal, got out of his car, and stepped onto the side of the road. The deah didn't move. The reverend moved a little closer. The deah didn't move. He plucked some dead grass, thinking: "This creature is so tame, maybe I can feed it." He moved closer still.

From the silence of evening came the blare of a bullhorn: "Step away from the decoy."

It was a fake deah set up by Fish and Game to catch jackers—those who illegally hunt deah at night. Even in deah season, you can't hunt deah in the dark.

Oh, deah.

death wahmed ova

A sickly state

"He looked like death wahmed ova—skinny, peak-id, shaky, eyes like cane holes in a cow flap."

"What ails him?"

"Red Sox lost to the Yankees."

deep South

Nashua, N.H.

To people from the North Country, though, it's actually any place south of Concord.

Democrat brownies

Rich chocolate dessert squares

At the polls in Northwood each year, the Harvey Lake Women's Club provides food. Jean makes lemonade and brownies, some marked Republican and some marked Democrat. I asked her the difference. She said, "The Democrat brownies are the ones with the nuts."

diarear

Looseness in the bowels

Friday brought torrential rain. Only about half the kids showed up to school. On Monday, the teacher received a note: "Miss

Pierce, please excuse Georgie from missing school on Friday. He had diarear and his boots leaked."

dicka
Negotiate price

At yahd sales, people are almost always willing to dicka.

diff'rent
Unusual

If we don't like something but prefer not to say so right out, we say, "It's diff'rent."

"How do you like my spider tattoo, Mimi?"

"It's diff'rent."

Eight generations of the Nelson family lived on the same patch of land. The old folks moved to Fryeburg, Maine, and when they returned for a visit, the young folks were some proud of having painted the house as promised. "What do you think?" they asked.

Pa said, "It's diff'rent."

Ma said, "We didn't know you were going to paint it yellow."

dinah
A small restaurant sometimes housed in a retired train car

If tripe and corn chowder (pronounced *con chowdah*) are on the menu, and you can get your egg sandwich either Eastern- or Western-style, you're probably at a dinah. Dig in.

dingle
Roads that interconnect, forming a loop

"Evenings we take a walk around the dingle to stay in shape."

dink

Someone you don't like

The irate driver says, "That dink cut me off."

dinnah

The noontime meal

The evening meal is suppah. This can confuse those unfamiliar with the tradition.

"Thought you said you were coming for dinnah, Iris? We waited until twelve-thirty, but by then we were all so hungry we had to eat. I hope you didn't get into an accident?"

"We figured dinnah would be around six, and we'd wheel in around five-thirty."

"Gawd, Iris, we usually eat breakfast between six-thirty and seven."

"I meant six tonight."

"Oh. You're coming for suppah then? It'll be pickup. Hope that's okay?"

Note: Thanksgiving dinnah and Christmas dinnah are always dinnah no matter what time you eat. If it's turkey and fixin's, it's dinnah.

dint

Short for didn't, which is short for did not

"You ate the last cookie."

"No, I dint."

dip

A quick swim, the only kind possible in the Atlantic Ocean off our short coast, where the water temperature might break 60 degrees in August

dipstick

1. Used to measure oil in a car engine

2. A person who lacks common sense

"He run out of gas halfway to Claremont. I told him the gas gauge was broke. The dipstick."

directions

A game played by locals at the expense of visitors

Nothing locals enjoy more than strangers asking directions

A stranger in a convertible asked Dick, "Is this the road to Mont Vernon?"

"Ayuh," Dick said.

Stranger took off in the direction of Francestown. Returned an hour later, mad as hell.

Dick said, "You didn't ask me which way."

Another stranger says, "What's the best way to get to Pinkham Notch?"

"Depends where you staht."

dite

More than a smidge, less than a scoach; just a little bit

A dite of red pepper is almost always too much.

If you're a dite touched in the head, you're weird.

doah

An entrance, usually hinged

Some old houses have a lot of them, as in this story from Kenneth Reid about his Springfield neighbor, Lena, who—even in her 80s—dint miss a trick:

Just after we had bought our old house, I looked out my window to see Lena standing behind someone who was working on the house with me. She was just standing there, watching as he worked away. I went to the porch and said "Hi, Lena."

She slowly looked up at me and asked: "What's he doing?"

I answered: "Scraping the old paint off that doah."

She: "Why's he doing that?"

Me: "So the new paint will stick better."

She: "He going to do that to all the doahs in the house?"

Me: "Probably."

She: "All thirteen of them?"

Me: "Lena, how did you know there are thirteen doahs in our house?"

She: "Well, there used to be fourteen 'til you took one out of the kitchen."

doah yahd

Means front yard, or back yard, or side yard; it's the space outside the doah you use the most

One lady said the first time she heard the term she thought it was a place to store doors, as in lumberyard.

doah-yahd call

A visit in the doah yahd

Pull in with your cah, roll down the window, exchange pleasantries with whoever emerges from the house. It's less of a commitment than going to the doah and knocking, though some doah-yard calls go on for a good long while.

Similiar is the standing-in-the-doah call. In this case, the visitor—usually uninvited—stands just inside the doah for the duration, refusing to take a seat or have a drink. Standing-in-the-doah calls can last two or three hours. Every half-hour or so the visitor reaches for the knob, then pulls back when he thinks of something else to say.

Dr. Green's

Liquor store

After Prohibition, all liquor in New Hampshire was sold at state-owned stores painted green. Refined folks would say, "I'm making a trip to Laconia tomorrow. Will you be needing anything from Dr. Green's?"

doctorin'

Seeing a doctor or visiting a medical facility

"Tuesday I went to the doctor about my bad back. Wednesday I got my blood sucked. Friday, I had to go back to see what the doctor thought of the numbers from the blood test. All that doctorin's enough to make you sick."

Dolly Copp

Early women's libber

Dolly Emery married Hayes Copp in 1831. She and Hayes lived in a remote part of the White Mountains, where they raised four children. Dolly was famous for her self-reliance, handiwork, and tiny feet. According to the story, on Dolly and Hayes's 50th wedding anniversary, she announced, "Fifty years is long enough to live with any man."

Then she walked, on those tiny feet, right out the door.

The Dolly Copp Campground bears her name.

Donor Town

Highly taxed towns; New Hampshire's tax system is so screwed up, we're forever trying to fix it—without much luck so far.

One of the brainstorms was to have rich towns pay extra for education to help out poor towns.

In Hebron, I asked, "What do you call yourselves? Hebroners? Hebronites?"

"Nope," they said. "Donor Town."

don't make yourself shot

Be sure not to give away money that you might need later on.

"Let me pay the toll since you're driving, Letty."

"Oh, no."

"I insist."

"All right, but don't make yourself shot."

don't that float ya boat?

Ain't that wonderful?

One of many sayings used by Joel Sherburne—native, cheese man, and the radio voice for Calef's Country Store in Barrington, where Joel has been waxing philosophical for more than 50 years.

Other Joelisms: Don't that make your livuh quiver? Meaning, kinda scary, eh? And, Don't that churn your buttah? Meaning, don't that kinda piss you off?

don't think so, me

A gentle way of disagreeing

"It's no more than an hour to Manchester."

"Don't think so, me. Construction on 93. Better allow an hour and a half."

down cellah

Into the basement

We go down cellah but not up attic.

down Eastuh

Someone from Maine with a funny accent

"I couldn't understand a word that fella said!"
"He's from Frenchboro."
"Oh. That explains it."

down Maine

A large state to the north and east of us

A native who'd spent a good deal of her life in California returned to New Hampshire in retirement. She vowed not to fall back into her native accent, as it had been the subject of ridicule in California, where, with much effort, she'd learned to speak as Californians speak.

Her first weekend back in the state, she took a trip down Maine in search of a lobster dinner at York Harbor. When she returned, she said: "It was a great trip. You can't get lobstah any freshah than Yawk Beach."

down street

Direction

In Danbury, where I spent a lot of time as a kid at my grand-parents' house on High Street, we'd go down street for milk or bread or sometimes a Popsicle.

Down street consisted of a cluster of buildings—the post office, Hastings's store, Gardner's store, and Hippie Hill (we steered clear of that) across from Gardner's store.

Related terms include up street and over street, also referring to making one's way to the village. If you live downhill from the village, you'd have to go up street to collect your mail. Kathy Smith grew up on the Bog in Penacook, so everywhere was up street for her. If you live near the village, but on the same plateau, you go over street.

down the road a piece

Not far, but not close either

In 1966 the senior class at Hollis High School took a field trip to Washington, D.C. A couple of the students met another couple in the elevator of their hotel.

"Where'd you go to suppah?" the first couple asked.

"Down the road a piece." Directions that might be helpful in Hollis, but not so great in Washington, D.C.

(*Down the Road a Piece* is also the title of John McDonald's *Storyteller's Guide to Maine.* Evidently, the expression spans the border.)

dragass

Helpful liquid

The lawn mower wouldn't start after a long Dalton winter. The neighbor, handy, suggested dragass.

"Dragass?" Angel said. She and her sister, Cathy, had retired to New Hampshire from away.

"I got dragass in my trunk. I'll go get it," the neighbor said.

"Dragass?"

"A dose of dragass, that mower will be running like a chahm."

"Dragass?"

"That's right."

"Spell it."

"D-R-Y G-A-S."

draw

1. Sometimes pronounced drawr—*to make a picture with a pencil, crayons, and the like*

2. To inhale, as in draw a breath

3. A bureau has draws for storing clothes. Among those clothes might be some underwear, also known as draws or underdrawrs.

Pearl lived next door to Leo. One day Pearl asked Leo to take a look at her desk. One of the draws was sticking. Later, talking with a neighbor, Pearl said: "That Leo," she said, "he's been fooling around with my draws all day!"

dressin'

Manure

In spring farmers dress their fields with dressin' so the crops will flourish.

Some farmers sell manure by grade, according to how long you've lived in town and how well you fit in. New people get the fresh stuff, which, though fragrant, can burn your tender plants. But if you've been around a while, he'll fill your bucket with the good stuff, high-test, the well-aged dressin'. When that happens you've passed the sniff test. Oh yes—New Hampshire, like any other place, has its own class system.

drive careful

A common farewell; good-bye, and, if all goes well, we'll see you later

dropped egg

Poached egg

Makes a good breakfast or suppah. "The chicken wa'n't unthawed, so Ada and Ellen whipped up some dropped eggs on toast."

druthahs

Preference

"Given our druthahs, we'd drink Moxie rather than cola."

dry

A town is dry if there's no liquor to be bought within its limits.

dry as a faht

A storyteller who delivers dry humor without so much as cracking a smile is said to be dry as a faht

dry humor

Funny stories delivered deadpan

Susan from Connecticut moved to New Hampshire as a preschooler. In first grade, the other children made fun of her Connecticut accent so she worked hard to talk like the others. And now, more than 50 years later, she could pass for a native. For years, she practiced dry Yankee humor on a coworker. He never laughed at her delivery of such lines as, "You can't get they-ah from he-ah."

Finally, on one red-letter day, he broke his silence and laughed out loud, quickly covering his mouth. He said, "Sorry, Susan. I couldn't help it. Sometimes the things you say are funny."

dry-ki

Dry, weathered wood; barkless limbs from long-dead trees

"The ice had coated everything. When we tried to make a campfire, not even the dry-ki would burn. 'Bout froze."

dub

To stay busy while accomplishing nothing much

"What're you going to do this afternoon?"
"I think I'll just dub around in the garage, sorting nails."

dubba

Someone who dubs around; a person who's lazy, incompetent, or both

"Gina's cousin offered to paint my house for five dollars an hour."

"He's a dubba. It'll cost you more in the long run than if you hired somebody decent for twice as much."

dumber'n a bag of hammers

Below-average intelligence

"Gina's cousin offered to rewire the electric on the camp real cheap."

"I wouldn't chance it. He's dumber'n a bag of hammers. That dubba couldn't wire his way out of a paper bag."

dump

1. Transfer station

2. What you deposit at the station for transfer

3. The act of depositing discards at the tranfer station

One dumps one's dump at the dump.

I'm told the Wilton Transfer Station had more than 50 stations for transferring various kinds of dump. Some things, however, weren't allowed. The sign read: THE WILTON TRANSFER STATION IS NOT AUTHOR-IZED TO ACCEPT FIREARMS. BUT INDIVIDUALS CAN, SO PLEASE ASK.

At the Northwood dump, a sign at the entrance read: IF IN DOUBT AS TO WHERE TO PUT IT, ASK ATTENDANT.

No doubt the dump master, if asked, would have been delighted to tell you exactly where to put it.

dump master

The man or woman in charge of the dump

Muriel took a rug, eight-by-ten, rolled it up, tied it off, and hauled it to the dump.

The dump master said, "You can't dump that."

"What?"

"You can't dump that rug today!"

"Why not?"

"Nothin' longer than foah feet allowed in the crusha."

So Muriel laid the rug out, sliced it down the middle, rolled the two halves back up, tied them off, and dumped them, while the dump master looked on, none too pleased.

dump picker

Someone skilled in finding usable merchandise among the refuse

Dump picking is illegal in some towns, so the dump master gets dibs.

Dump pickers refer to the town dump as the Country Store, the Warehouse, or the Outdoor Market.

A trip to the dump was (and is) my family's idea of an outing. One time my dad was looking particularly dapper. I complimented his outfit.

He said: "All from the Country Store—jacket, shirt, pants, and shoes."

"I guess you draw the line at underwear and socks," I said.

"No," he said. "Couldn't find any."

Course, you can get carried away with dump picking. Rule of thumb: Don't take home more than you deposit.

dynamite pills

Strong medicine designed to knock the hell out of what ails ya

"Doc told me to take three dynamite pills a day for ten days. So I did."

"How do you feel?"

"If I felt any bettah, I'd be twins."

eat with a spoon

An expression of affection

"Grandma said she loved Grandfather so much when they first married she could have eaten him with a spoon. Fifty years later, she wished she had."

elastic

Rubber band

The teacher sent her assistant, a young woman from the South (Connecticut, I think), to her desk to fetch elastics out of the left top draw.

The aide returned frustrated—couldn't find any. All the draw contained was staples, paper clips, note cards, and a box of rubber bands.

electrifried

Shocked or electrocuted

"Ellis grabbed ahold of that live wire and electrifried himself."
"Did he have to go to the hospital?"
"No. But it got his attention for a minute or two."

elegant

Very fine; a successful effort

"How'd your colonoscopy go, Ollie?"
"Elegant."

empty the teakettle

An elegant way to describe a visit to the ladies' room

"Excuse me, girls. I need to empty the teakettle."

enuffa

Plenty of

"Children, stop your fighting. That's enuffa that."

epizudic

Flu

"Wally and Jill would have been here for the ribbon cutting, but Jill had the epizudic and thought it best to keep her germs in the family."

et

Eat or ate

Bob Ramsay of Alexandria told about Gus, who took a mortgage out on a heifer in the amount of $10, borrowed from his neighbor, Joel Gray.

One day Joel come traipsing down the hill. He stopped by Gus's fahm. Joel said: "Gus, you owe me ten dollars for the mortgage on that white-faced heifer."

Gus cackled. "Ha," he said. "I done fooled you. I et that heifer."

Joel reached into his pocket with his monstrous dairy-farmer hand. He pulled out a slip of paper pinched between two monstrous fingers and said, "But you didn't et the mortgage."

Great-Grandma sealed the floor of the outhouse with benzene. Great-Grampa enjoyed a smoke as he set. He tapped out the ashes from his pipe on the benzene-soaked floor. Next thing he knew he was in the duck pond. When he surfaced he said, "What the hell I et?"

exciting as cold dishwater

Gray, wet, uninspiring

"That speech was about as exciting as cold dishwater."

In Durham they tell of the visiting pastor, boarding at a local farm. Sunday morning, Mrs. French made a big breakfast, which the pastor declined, saying he preached better on an empty stomach. Mr. French and the preacher went off to church, while Mrs. French stayed home to cook Sunday dinner.

When Mr. French and the preacher returned, Mrs. French took her husband aside to inquire, discreetly, how the service had gone. Mr. French said: "He shoulda et."

eyes like peeled onions

Bulging eyes indicating surprise or shock

"When the pork roast fell onto the floor, that dog froze and his eyes stuck out like peeled onions."

eyes like two cane holes in a cow flap

A person with such eyes needs a long nap, chicken soup, or some doctorin

True story: Dr. Clough took care of most everybody in town. A hermit who lived on the side of the mountain normally walked down to the village every couple of weeks for supplies, but nobody'd seen him for a month. Dr. Clough decided to trek out to the hermit's place to see what was up. He took his young son with him (a boy who would later become the second Dr. Clough).

When they got to the remote cabin, the doors and windows were locked tight from the inside. Dr. Clough hollered but received no answer. He spotted a high window open a crack. Hoisted his son on his shoulders. The boy squeezed through the window and dropped to the floor. There sat the hermit in a rocking chair, eyes like two cane holes in a cow flap, and a shotgun trained on the young intruder.

The boy explained that he'd come with his dad to help.

The hermit indicated that the boy might open the door and let Dr. Clough in.

"I'm real sick," the hermit said. "I think I'm done for."

The doctor looked him over. "I don't think you're done for. I think you need an enema."

The enema was duly administered, and the hermit felt immediate relief.

"How much do I owe you, Doc?"

"Well," the doctor said, "it took me half the day to walk out here, and it'll take the other half to walk back. How about five dollars?"

The hermit handed him a $10 bill. He said, "That first one felt so good, Doc, I'll have another."

F

faggot

A twig; a person gathers faggots for kindling.

My grandmother always did. She'd bring in a few faggots every morning to get the stove in the kitchen going. The woods around her house were easy walking, because after decades of faggot collecting, she'd tidied them up.

fahm

Land used for agriculture

In 1900, New Hampshire was mostly fahms, separated by stone walls and hardly any trees. Now it's just the opposite. Once you get outside the big cities like Dover, Portsmouth, Nashua, and Manchester, it's woods, woods, and more woods. If you walk in the woods, you'll stumble over the stone walls and cellar holes, reminders of what used to be.

"How does a fahmah get a million dollars?"

"He stahts with two million."

faht

To pass gas. Toot. A reverse belch. Past tense: fahted. Past perfect: have fahted. Progressive: is fahting. Future: will faht. Future perfect progressive: will have been fahting.

Often associated with eating and digesting beans or other legumes; hence, the children's rhyme that begins, "Beans, beans, the musical fruit."

fatha

Married to muhtha; male parent of sista and bruhtha

fawk

A table setting consists of a fawk, spoon, and knife.

Roland had the unusual habit of eating ice cream with a fawk. One evening, enjoying a bowl, he dropped the fawk and it stuck into his foot, the tines drawing blood.

His wife said, "Roland, have you learned anything from this?"

He said, "Yes. Wear shoes when I'm eating ice cream."

fayuh

1. If you win without cheating, that's fayuh.

2. Weather can be fayuh or fowull.

3. It's fun to go to the fayuh, see the livestock, eat cotton candy, and ride the teacups.

Perry Sawyer's brother entered his team of oxen in the pulling contest at the fayuh. When he got home, Father asked how he did.

Brother says, "We come in next to top."

The neighbor, Hugh Dunning, also had a team of oxen. "How'd Hugh do?"

"He come in next to last."

"How many teams?"

"Two."

fella

A male person

fence viewer

Town official in charge of looking at fences to help settle boundary disputes

Fence viewing is considerably more exciting than watching grass grow.

fie-uh

Flame

Woofy, the youngest of five children, didn't speak as a toddler until well past the age when maybe he should have had something to say. His folks wondered if there might be something wrong with the little fella. Maybe, though, he didn't talk because his brothers and sisters talked so much he didn't need to.

One day, when the others were in school, Woofy's mother was stoking the fie-uh in the cookstove. She put in some small wood and got that going. Then she tried to put a piece of chunk wood on top. She lifted one cast-iron lid and tried to shove the wood in. Then another lid. Tried different angles. Meanwhile, the kindling started shooting flames and the chunk wood wedged stuck, fie-uh flaring around it and smoke billowing.

Woofy, from his little chair in the corner, said: "'T'won't go, Ma. Too goddam big."

His first words!

fie-uh depahtment

Just about every town has a fie-uh depahtment and a fie-uh station or two with pumpah trucks sent out when somebody's place catches fie-uh. Many towns now pay professional fie-uh fighters helped out by volunteers.

In Plainfield, Ellsworth Atwood called in a fie-uh at his farm, way back in the boondocks.

"The bahn's on fie-uh," he said.

The professional fie-uh fighter, recently moved to town from away, said: "How do we get there?"

Ellsworth said, "You still got those big red trucks?"

71

fillin' station

Gas station

Years ago, fillin' stations sold just one thing: gas. A game warden (pronounced *wahdin*) spent a good deal of his time maintaining order in the wilds of the North Country, and one dismal, foggy morning, early, he was fillin' his tank at a fillin' station. Also at the pump was an old fella fillin' the tank of his pickup truck. The warden and the old fella stood on either side of the pump, not saying a word to one another, in the Yankee tradition.

Finally, the warden said out loud: "I wonder where a fella can get a good cup of coffee around here this time of the day."

The old fella took a draw off his pipe, pulled it from his mouth, and set it carefully on the roof of his pickup.

"Well, sir," he said. "I guess you'll just have to come home with me."

first-in-the-nation primary

Every four years, the candidates for President of the United States descend on New Hampshire to make their cases. Our primary is held before primaries in any other states. Why? Because that's the way it's always been done. And because it's the law. Long ago, our legislature passed a law saying our primary would be held at least seven days before any other similar election. And that's that.

Originally and traditionally, primary day is the second Tuesday in March, but we've been holding them earlier on account of some other states trying to sneak their primaries in before us. We won't have it. In 2007, we held the primary on the 8th of January. Had to. Pesky Michigan set theirs for the 15th. If we have to hold the primary on New Year's Day—or Christmas, for that matter—we will. Make no mistake about it.

fish cop

A conservation officer

Years ago the salmon (prounUnced *sal-mon* in Berlin, *sammin* in the rest of the state) used to run heavy up the Cockermouth River into Newfound Lake. Of course, when the sammin were running upriver to spawn, you couldn't fish for them. Wouldn't have been fayuh. They had their minds on other things.

A fish cop was poking around near the river when he heard gunfire. He headed in that direction and come upon Old Brad sitting on the bank with a .22 across his knees.

"What are you doing?" the fish cop asked.

"Shootin' mushrats."

The fish cop looked and beyond Old Brad in the ferns he spotted three beautiful big sammin, all laid out, not looking too lively. "Shooting mushrats, huh!" he said.

"Ayuh. Scaley buggers, ain't they?"

flatlander

Someone from a land less hilly or mountainous than ours

For many in northern New England, a flatlander is someone from Rhode Island, Connecticut, or Massachusetts. For those in New Hampshire who live in the White Mountains region, a flatlander is anyone who lives south of the notches. And for those hardy few who man the observatory on top of Mount Washington, a flatlander is everybody else.

floundrin'

Floppin' around like a fish on a deck

"Chuck stahted a new business selling chain-saw carvings to tourists."

"How's he doing?"

"Floundrin'. He tried making bear statues, moose statues, totem poles, moose, but they all look like mushrooms."

flume

A passage through rocks and ledge carved by a brook

In Franconia Notch, The Flume is a popular tourist attraction. In high school, my friend Pat Huckins and I thought it would be a good idea to hike a mountain and camp overnight. It was August, wahm. We didn't bring a tent, just sleeping bags. All went well, until in the middle of the night, it started to rain. We lay out on a ledge, bundled in our sleeping bags, and braved the torrent.

Next day, our packs soaked, our sleeping bags soaked and weighing about 100 pounds, us soaked and bedraggled, we took the shortcut down through The Flume, where we encountered tourists in sundresses and sandals. We must have looked like death wahmed over. One tourist asked us how long we'd been in the mountains. We said: "One night."

That was plenty.

4,000-footer club

Nothing at all like the mile-high club, just sayin'. People who belong to the 4,000-footer club have climbed all 48 of New Hampshire's mountains higher than 4,000 feet.

fox

1. A small dog-like animal with a pointy nose and an appetite for rabbits and house cats

If a fox gets too friendly, cowt, it might have the rabies. The rabies is not something you want to get exposed to, because it'll kill you unless you take the shots.

Michelle Hernandez saw a fox sneak into her back yard, grab the red ball that belonged to her Jack Russell terrier, and run off with it. Pretty cute! But who's going to throw the ball for that fox?

2. The plural of tined cutlery that partners with spoons and knives at suppah

When your host asks, "Would you please get the fox out of the draw," don't be looking around for a furry mammal; set the table.

3. A split in the road

"Where the road fox, I saw a muhtha fox and three kits. Wa'n't they cunnin'."

Translation: "Where the road forks, I saw a mother fox and three babies. They were adorable."

fox pox
Faux pas; a slip of the tongue or action that causes embarrassment

Linda is a Questor—a member of a group of preservationists and collectors. At a large antiques flea market, she ran into a longtime acquaintance. "How are you doing?" she asked.

"Well," he said, "I lost my wife."

"I'm sure you'll find her," Linda said. "I'm always losing my husband at these flea markets."

The man explained that his wife had, in fact, died.

Fox pox.

At a prestigious college, smoodging at a party before performing some stories, I got talking with a nice woman—well-dressed, tasteful jewelry, perfect makeup (the opposite of me). We hit it off. After a while I said, "Do you work here?"

"Yes."

"What do you do?"

"I'm the president."

Fox pox.

frappe

I don't know what these thick beverages are called in other parts of the country, but here, a frappe is milk, syrup, and ice cream beaten together.

A milk shake is milk, syrup, no ice cream. A hoss's neck is ice cream and soda, usually Pepsi; least it was at my house—a favorite after-school treat. Sometimes we got salt and peppered potato slices, too. Raw. Nawthin' better and better than nawthin'.

Swamp water was another old-time fountain favorite: half orange tonic and half root beer.

Free Staters

People from away who belong to the Free State Project and choose to move to New Hampshire because it's the Live Free or Die state

Free Staters despise taxes and like guns. Their plan—I know this because I checked the website—is to move into small towns where a few people (them) voting as a block can take over town government. Naturally some of the natives take umbrage at this taking-over business. Thing is, the Free Staters look and act like everybody else, so they blend right in. Maybe they have come to the right place after all.

fresh out

Just sold, gave away, lost, or buried the last one

"How's your wife, Lyle?"

"To tell you the truth, I'm fresh out."

frickin'

An amplifier

Frickin' potato bugs are more voracious than plain old potato bugs.

"We usually go to the Deerfield Fair on Thursday or Friday because it's so frickin' crowded on the weekend."

frig

To screw up, mess up, or dub around with; also, frigs, frigged, friggin'

When a person who doesn't know what he's doing frigs with the friggin' settin's on the cable box, the television gets all frigged up.

from away

Not from here; some are more from away than others

"You the new people in town?"

"Yes. We moved down from Maine."

"But you ain't from there, are ya?"

In Colebrook at a church supper, a local took pity on a couple from away, sitting all by themselves. She struck up a conversation. The couple said they'd moved to Colebrook from Colorado earlier in the month.

The local said, "See that woman in the white sweater over by the coffeepot? You have a lot in common with her. She's also new in town and from out West."

The couple approached the woman in the white sweater: "Nettie told us you were new in town and from out West."

The woman said, "I've lived here seven years and I'm from Vermont."

At the dedication of the new ballpark, Sara remarked: "Just think, I've lived in this town twenty-five years."

Justine said, "And we're just stahting to get used to you."

front doah

By tradition, the front doah on an old colonial home is opened only for weddings and funerals. It's a wide doah, so the coffin can pass through freely.

frost heave

A dip in the road caused by the buildup and subsequent melting of ice under the tar

The town and the state mark these with signs reading FROST HEAVE. If you see a sign that says, BUMP, that's a whopper of a frost heave. We had one in front of our house last spring, and those vehicles that failed to heed the warning left parts behind. I piled the bits and pieces of metal, along with one spare tire, a bumpa, and a tailpipe, on the lawn and called it sculptcha.

The classic story goes like this: The newspaper reporter from New York City calls town hall in a small North Country town to do research on the presidential primary. The reporter asks the town clerk, "Who's winning?"

"How should I know?" the clerk says.

"Well," the reporter says, "who's got the most campaign signs along the road?"

"Oh," the clerk said, "that would be Frost Heaves."

frugal

Careful with money

A true Yankee will squeeze a penny until old Abe's head turns blue and he cries out for mercy.

Jenny looked over the cheeses at the market. She loved Swiss, but it was $5.99 a pound and mostly holes, so, being frugal, she bought the cheddar instead.

Some of us take frugality about as far as it can go. We save our bacon grease in a jar, so we need never buy olive oil—which, if you notice, is pretty pricey.

When Ellis made tea, he'd measure the exact amount of water needed in his teacup, then pour it into the kettle to boil. He was also a great one for composting, including tea bags. He'd remove the paper tag, burn it in the woodstove, and compost the rest.

A family in Barrington peeled the labels from the empty cans of soup or beans and saved them for lighting the woodstove. (So do I, come to think of it.)

full chisel

Using all available power; also, full bore, using all the firepower a gun can muster

After driving more than seven hours from Connecticut during a nor'easter, Bing, Jill, and the kids were almost to the old home place, when they got stuck halfway up the big hill. Bing said to Jill: "Rev her up full chisel and I'll push."

The car started to move. Hurrah! Bing thought. Then he saw the brake lights, 50 yards up the hill. She'd stopped so he could catch up and jump in. And they were stuck again.

A four-wheel-drive come up the hill behind them at a good clip, pulled around the stuck vehicle, and continued on. Bing recognized his mother-in-law's vehicle. Guess we're gonna be late for supper, he thought.

G

gahdin

1. Something prisoners need so they don't escape

2. A fertile plot for growing vegetables, herbs, and flowers

Some people have such big gahdins you wonder what they do with all that produce. They say: "We eat what we can, and what we can't, we can."

Kenneth Reid was working in his gahdin one Sunday when his octogenarian neighbor got home from church.

Kenneth said, "Hi, Lena. Many at church this morning?"

She said: "Eight—if you'd been there."

gahdin hackle

A fly-fishing term for mud worms

gainin'

Making progress, recovering from an illness or accident

"How's Mildred doing since her shock?"

"She's gainin'."

gallunkin'

Trolling for fish with a sinking fly, lure, or live bait

For gallunkin' you use a gallunkin' pole, stiffer than a spinnin' rod and equipped with many colors of lead line—well, it's not really lead, but it's heavy, so it sinks. The more colors of line you let out, the deeper the lure goes. If you know how deep the fish are, you let out the appropriate number of colors.

"Going out on the pond this evening gallunkin'."

"How many colors?"

"Six or seven."

"Sounds about right."

gaw

An expression of surprise or disappointment, more often heard on the seacoast—Seabrook in particular—than inland

While hunting ducks, Pete drank to ward (pronounced *wad*) off the damp. He and Warren had been sitting in the blind quite a while, warming themselves with spirits, so Pete was pretty well tuned when a duck flew overhead. He raised his shotgun and blasted the duck, which fell into the pond, *kersplash*. Pete seemed disappointed though.

"What's the matter, Pete?"

"Gaw, Warren," he said. "I usually get two or three out of a flock that size."

gawm

Sticky situation; big mess

"Godfrey mighty, that's some gawm, them hawgs rootin' up your whole gahdin like that."

"Wouldn't be so bad if they wa'n't my ex-wife's new boyfriend's muhtha's hawgs."

gawmin

Impressively larger than average

"That center on the basketball team is gawmin, and so's her sister, Natalie."

At the lumber camp, newcomer Andre, after a hard day's work, took a seat in a gawmin rocking chair by the stove. "Don't sit in that chair," a colleague warned.

"Why not?"

"That's Ola's chair."

81

"Don't have Ola's name on it."

In come Ola, a great gawmin lumberjack, looking none too pleased.

Andre jumped up quick. "Here's your chair, Ola. Just keeping it wahm for you."

gawry
Surely; golly; oh, my; expresses surprise or consternation

"Gawry, you must have been some scared when that ladder collapsed."

"Ayuh. That was some hairy ride off the roof and into the rhodydendrum, bettah b'lieve it."

Variation: By gawry. It's true.

"In high school band we had to wear white shoes," Roger said. "So, by gawry, I painted my brown ones."

get the derrick
Help

After a big meal, my maternal grandmother, Lillian Grace Stewart, would say, "Get the derrick," meaning she'd eaten so much she couldn't rise from her seat on her own. We'd have to bring in the heavy equipment and cables to stand her upright.

ginnegar
Combines ginger and vinegar

Not a beverage but a show of strength or energy.

If the hired hand put a little more ginnegar into swinging that scythe, he'd finish his mowing sooner. Baseball pitchers whose throws are being hit regularly by the batters might need a little more ginnegar on the ball. A losing throw of the dice reveals insufficient ginnegar.

glacial erratic

When the glacier went through, it picked up boulders and deposited them in strange places.

A huge boulder (by huge, I mean bigger than an elephant) standing alone or alone with a few big friends that don't match the other rocks in the area is likely a glacial erratic. We name them. There's the Bartlett Boulder, Frog Rock in New Boston, the Glen Boulder, the Madison Boulder, Boise Rock, and many others.

After a walk out the trail to visit the Madison Boulder, the lady from away said, "It's certainly impressive, but I don't know why they couldn't have put it closer to the road."

At my grandparents' house on Waukeena Lake Road in Danbury stands an unnamed glacial erratic, bigger than the house. A traveling salesman asked my paternal grandmother—Elizabeth Moynihan Barker, originally from Galway, Ireland—how that big rock came to be there. She said, "I don't know. 'Twas here when I arrived."

Glaciers left small rocks as well as big ones. The fella from away spots the farmer picking rocks out of his field and piling them. "How'd all those rocks get in your field?" the fella asks.

Farmer says, "The glacier brought them."

Fella says, "Where's the glacier now?"

Farmer says, "Guess it went back for another load."

glare ice

A coating of ice on the road that makes steering next to impossible

The worst thing you can do on glare ice is hit the brakes. I know. I've done it. And spun all the way around. Not the 180, but the full 360. At the Lee traffic circle. Wa'n't I scay-ed.

glom

Hold tight or stay close

"When Hector spotted the pretty girl at the dance, he wanted to glom right onto her. And he did."

glovy hole

The opening in a pipe through which a glassblower blows glass

Sometimes in August, the weather gets hotter than a glovy hole. Out West, in places like Death Valley, seems like it's always hotter than a glovy hole.

goat eggs

No such thing; something that doesn't exist, though some folks might imagine it does

When something's scarce as goat eggs it's even scarcer than hen's teeth.

Caleb, ten, who helps out on the family goat farm, got a kick out of the lady from away who noticed cartons of eggs in the refrigerator case at the farm shop. She said to her son, "Look, they even have goat eggs."

goddamredsox

A one-word expletive naming the baseball team from Boston when it loses

Ned says he never owned a television until "the Red Sox started to do a little better." Probably applies to a lot of people.

godfrey mighty

Gosh!

"Godfrey mighty," Maybeth said. "Company's coming and there's a goat in the parlor refusing to leave."

gone to pot

Rendered useless through neglect, misuse, or mistreatment

"Didn't you used to have a riding lawnmower?"

"Lent it to Toby. Nimrod left it out all winter and it's gone to pot."

goodnuf

Adequate

"How is Polly at diggin' holes?"

"Goodnuf."

goodnyou

Polite response to "Howahya?"

goofer

White Mountains tourist

"And then the goofer asked how old a deah had to be before it turned into a moose."

goo-wd

Good; a fine all-purpose word pronounced with two syllables in pockets of New Hampshire, especially in the north

"Is the milk still goo-wd?"

"I b'lieve so."

"Oh, geez, it's not goo-wd. It's turned."

gracious

An exclamation expressing amazement; also goodness gracious, expressing even more amazement

"Gracious, that's a big rock."

"Why, that's not just a rock, Lil, it's a glacial erratic."

"Goodness gracious, that's a fancy name. What's it mean?"

"Big rock."

granite

A type of rock; New Hampshire has a lot of it, so we're called the Granite State.

When Nona woke up from surgery, the doctor told her he'd removed three stones from her gallbladder.

"Were they New Hampshire granite?" she asked.

Holly told this story in Wolfeboro. She and her family spent time each summer at some rental cabins on Lake Winnipesaukee. The recreation area was surrounded by big rocks, which Holly found hard to maneuver because she has cerebral palsy. The owners of the cabins were very accommodatin', she said. They built a rail along the rickety steps to her cabin to make getting in and out easier.

"Is there anything else we can do for you?" the owner asked her.

She said, "Could you do something about the rocks?"

"Well," he said, "you realize, this is the Granite State."

All these years later, she's still chuckling.

green around the gills

A sickly fish has a greenish hue in the gill area. A person whose tummy's upset may show some green coloration around her lips.

After Jessica got off the Tilt-A-Whirl at the Hopkinton Fair, she was staggering and green around the gills.

green tomato pie

Tastes just like it sounds

Since tomatoes don't ripen around here until August, some cooks get impatient and cook 'em green. Louise did. She served some to her husband, who said, "You needn't make that again for a while."

grinda

Submarine sandwich, hoagie, Italian sandwich

The lady from away said when she first ordered a grinda for lunch, she thought she was getting a ground-meat sandwich.

grunt

1. The noise pigs (and some people) make

2. A dessert made with berries

To make a grunt you simmer the blueberries, strawberries, raspberries, blackberries—whatever's in season—with sugar and water. When the berries are well and truly stewed, drop dumplin's on top and simmer some more. Great for summer days, when you don't want to heat up the kitchen by lighting the oven. Apple grunt is also an old-time favorite.

guess prob'ly

Dick Merrill of Berlin attributes this definition to his grandfather, Leonard Merrill: "When you guess prob'ly, you don't guess at all. You're pretty damn sure."

gumption

Spunk

"If he had any gumption at all, he'd stand up to that bigmouth boss of his."

H

hafassed

Poorly thought out or executed; inadequate

"Did Ronny fix the toilet?"

"He made a hafassed job of it. It flushes, occasionally, if you fiddle with the handle and say the magic words."

hahd

1. Not soft

"That mattress was so hahd, it was like sleeping on a bo-ahd."

2. Difficult

"Calculus is hahd to kellate."

3. Containing alcohol

"Hahd cider will make you drunk. Apple jack will make you drunker faster."

hahda than pissin' up a rope

Very difficult

h'ain't

Hasn't

"Perk must have some zucchini to spare. He put in twelve hills."

"Not this ye-ah, he h'ain't. Slugs got 'em."

Another year, when the slugs weren't so active, the story goes like this: Fella from away says, "Is it safe to leave my car unlocked on the street?"

"No it h'ain't," the local says. "Perk might come by and deposit some zucchini in your backseat."

handydowns

Secondhand clothes

Children from big families live in handydowns. One little girl, the youngest of five, didn't much mind wearing her sisters' used clothes. But for her eighth birthday, her mother splurged on a new dress from a Manchester department store. She wrapped the dress in tissue, put it in a box, wrapped the box, tied it with ribbon, and presented it to her daughter. The little girl took her time opening the gift. When she lifted the dress from the tissue she said, "Oh Mommy, it's beautiful. Whose was it?"

happast

Twelve-thirty is happast twelve. Two-thirty is happast two. And so on.

hawnet

A stinging insect

"Crossing the field, Laurette stepped on a hawnet's nest. Wa'n't they ugly? And dint she hightail it outta they-ah."

hawnpout or pout

A type of catfish that lives in lakes and ponds in New England

Their whiskers look like hawns, and their fins can cut you if you don't hold them just right. People fish for hawnpout at night by lantern light. The best bait for hawnpout is the night crawlah, but regular mud worms will work, too, if the pout are in a biting mood.

hawns

1. Antlers

Buck deah have hawns, but does don't.

2. The noisemakers on automobiles

Massachusetts drivers blow their hawns a lot. We don't know why.

headin' for the rhubarb

If a person is said to be headin' for the rhubarb, he or she is about to get into trouble.

"Don't let your wife sign up for that trip to the Foxwoods casino, Nute. There'll be drinkin', gamblin', and carousin'. She gets on that bus, she's headin' for the rhubarb."

heal like a dawg

Heal quickly

From Howard Chase: "One day John was odd-jobbing for one of the neighbors and knocked some hide off one of his knuckles. The woman he was working for offered to bandage the place, but John said, 'No, thank you; I heal up like a dawg.' "

heavy-lookin'-on

Observing

On a job site, some workers do the digging or the building or the directing of traffic, and others lean.

They are the ones in charge of the heavy-lookin'-on.

hedgehog

Porcupine

The second grade teacher asked her class if any of them had seen one in the wild. "No," said the little girl, "but my dog has."

hidebehind

Small animal

Cousin to the tree squeak, but slightly larger and with googly eyes. In the deep woods you can feel them looking at you, but you never see them. Not very good eating; too small and bony.

hideyhole

Dark hiding place

My cat, Rabies, likes to snuggle under the blanket in his little hideyhole.

hod

1. A pail for hauling coal

"Go down cellah and fill the hod, wouldja? We're gettin low on coal."

2. Strange or weird

"Raymond is kinda hod, h'ain't he?"
"That whole family's hod, if you ask me."

Hogan's goat

I've heard three usages: nastier than Hogan's goat, meaner than Hogan's goat, and number than Hogan's goat. Evidently, Hogan's goat was a winnah.

hog reeves

Elected town officials charged with controlling unruly hogs

In Dunbarton, by tradition, the hog reeves are the couple (or couple of couples) most recently married. They serve for a year. The fine for a loose hog in Dunbarton, still on the books, is 25 shillings (just under $3).

homely

An all-purpose term for something that's not pretty

"That pie was homely, but it tasted good."

Fella from the city visiting the farm says, "That's the homeliest dog I ever saw." He was looking at the goat.

Same fella, at dusk, looks out in the orchard. "That's the home-liest horse I ever saw." It was a moose.

homely as a bag of doorknobs

Extra homely

honey pot

The ceramic chamber pot in the commode by the bed, for use in the night, should nature call; also known as a honey bucket

honey wagon

A truck for hauling septage

The sign on the side of the honeywagon said, LULL'S SEPTIC: OUR BUSINESS SUCKS. Another reads, NUMBER 1 IN THE NUMBER 2 BUSINESS.

honkin'

Larger or more intense than expected

"That's some honkin' tomato. You oughta enter it in the Hopkinton fayuh."

"That honkin' sinus infection laid me out. I was sick a-bed in the wood box for two weeks."

hoozie

A person or thing whose proper name you can't recall; also, hoozie whatzit

"We'll never make it to church unless hoozie turns up in the next five minutes to plow us out."

hoozie whiskers

A person with a beard whose name you can't recall

"Where'd you get your grapevines?"
"Bought 'em off hoozie whiskers over Five Corners."

hoppa

Bigger than a trash basket or trash bucket; also called a bin

Might be one of those commercial haul-away bins parked outside condominiums or businesses.

"Mop's broke."

"Throw it in the hoppa."

Might be the crusha at the dump, also called a compactor, because when the dump master pulls the lever from inside his or her little dump-master cottage, the steel slabs hydraulic together and everything inside gets compacted.

"How did Grammie break her wrist?"

"She was throwing bags off the back of the truck, slipped, and fell into the hoppa."

"Jeesumcrow."

"That's what she said. Coulda been worse, though. Luckily, Kermit, the dump master, noticed her predicament and shut down the hydraulics right off quick."

hospice

Pronounced hoss piss, *it is a program to help people at the end of their lives.*

At town meeting, a woman spoke in favor of allocating $500 for hoss piss.

The farmer said, "I'm voting no. Got too much of that stuff rotting out my bahn floor already."

hoss

An animal for riding, racing, or pulling buggies

Cliff and Horace Colcord were bachelor brothers who lived together on the family homestead. One day a hoss and buggy went by as the brothers sat on the porch. "Ain't that a beautiful bay hoss," Cliff said to Horace.

A week passed.

Horace said to Cliff, "That wa'n't a bay hoss. It was a black."

Another week passed. Cliff appeared at the door with a satchel. "Where you going, Cliff?" Horace said.

"Movin' out," Cliff said. "Can't stand all this bickerin'."

hoss thieves

Means the opposite of what you might think. It's short for The Walpole Society for Bringing to Justice Horse Thieves and Pilferers of Clotheslines and Hen Roosts.

This is a group of men with a proud history of not doing very much at all. They did manage to return one hoss to its owner a few decades back, but it was dead. Now they hold a dinner every other year and invite a speaker. One year they invited me. They don't usually invite women speakers. Don't b'lieve they've invited another one since.

hots

Hot peppers

"You want hots on your grinda?"

"Nope. My ulcer won't stand for it."

hotter'n the hinges'a hell

Over 75 degrees Fahrenheit

"I had to lay down and take a nap with the fan blowing on me. It was hotter'n the hinges'a hell. And humid, too."

hot ticket

A person with spunk and initiative

"Aunt Myrna's getting married again. She's buried three husbands already, but that don't stop her. She's a hot ticket."

hotty quizeen

What the French spell haute cuisine—food served in a fancy place

Hotty quizeen is what they serve in the grand dining room at the Mount Washington Hotel, locally referred to as The Wash, a fancy place overlooking the beautiful Mount Washington Valley and Presidential Range.

A Texan, relaxing on The Wash's wide wraparound porch, famously said, "You'd have a good view from here, if them mountains weren't in the way."

One time my husband and I went with another couple to a very fancy restaurant known for its hotty quizeen. We enjoyed our meals, but stopped at McDonald's on the way home so we could get something to eat.

house room

Used in the expression "I wouldn't give it house room," meaning it's not worth the space it would occupy

At the auction, Tilly bid on a marble-top sideboard. Her friend said, "Tilly, what are you biddin' on that homely thing for? I wouldn't give it house room."

hummin'

1. Running smoothly

"Perley's 1938 ton-and-a-half dump truck with the flathead V-8 was just a hummin' after its tune-up."

2. Complaining

"Aunt Mehitabel tripped over the bicycle that Juniper left in the walkway. When she limped into the house, wa'n't she hummin'."

hump
Move quickly

"I better hump along home. It's suppah time."

hunker down
Concentrate and work hard to prepare

"We're never going to get them three cod of wood stacked if we don't hunker down."

"It ain't going to stack itself, that's for shoe-uh."

When we hear a hurricane or ice storm is coming, we hunker down.

huntin'
Seeking game for the purpose of killing and eating it

In New Hampshire, we hunt pattige, pheasant, woodcock, turkey, deah, bayuh, and moose. Huntin' takes skill and knowledge—plus you have to buy a license, or, in the case of moose, win a permit in the lottery.

Toad told Russell he was goin huntin' with Spike Grimes on Saturday, over to the meadow. Russell said: "Toad, I thought you said you'd never hunt with Spike Grimes agin?"

"He talked me into it. I don't know how. He's already shot me twice."

Hurricane of '38
The big blow of 1938 that did much damage up and down the East Coast

The storm is remembered by all who experienced it for its high winds and rain, roofs ripped off, and forests flattened.

Vea Jenks of Piermont sent this story, passed down from her mother:

During the hurricane an old farmer arose and began to dress.

"What you doin', Elmer?" his wife called from the bed.

"Dressin'," he said grimly. "This house may soon be blowed clear to the village. How you're goin' is your business. I'm a-goin' in my pants."

In Keene, after the worst of the storm, Howard Andros was walking up North Main Street. The trees were down everywhere, a big crisscrossed mess. He got to Cemetery Hill, where he met a local also picking his way through the rubble.

Howard said, "That was some blow."

The local said, "Ayuh. Wood'll be cheap this winter."

I, J, and K

I await your pleasure

What the moderator says at town or school meeting when the floor is open to a motion or a comment from the assembly

ice-out

When the ice on the lake has melted enough that the water is navigable

On Winnipesaukee, it's when the *Mount Washington* cruise ship can reach all its ports of call at Alton Bay, Center Harbor, Weirs Beach, Meredith, and Wolfeboro. Bets are taken on the exact day and time that ice-out will occur, as determined by an observer from Emerson Aviation doing a flyover.

ice storm

Doesn't rain ice, that would be a hailstorm; when the cold comes on top of rain and ice forms on everything—trees, wires, roofs, cars, driveways, roads—that's an ice storm. It can wreak havoc.

In 2008, an ice storm took out electricity in New Hampshire for two weeks or more. That's inconvenient, especially since a good many of us get water from wells with pumps, run by—you guessed it—electricity. Those lucky enough to have pitcher pumps had lots of company.

After one ice storm, I said to my daughter, who needed to be to work by noon, "You better start scraping your car if you plan to get to work on time. I just spent an hour scraping mine off."

She said, "Can I borrow your car?"

idear

A thought

In the Farmington parade, Walter drove his antique Packard. It was so hot, the Packard stalled. The parade halted. At the rear a tourist (probably from Massachusetts) tooted persistently, encouraging the stalled Packard and the stalled parade to proceed. Walter got out of the Packard, walked back to the tourist's car. "I got an idear," he said. "I'll set heah and blow your hawn and you go staht my car."

if I felt any better I couldn't stand it

A saying from Don Dollard's grandfather, which reflects the Yankee attitude of optimistic pessimism

if I felt any better I'd be twins

A cheerful Uncle George Radcliffe, Yankee storyteller from Webster, said this to me one time, and I never forgot it.

if you can't lick 'em, brick 'em

If you can't beat them one way, try an alternative.

if you don't know how to get here, you shouldn't come

Uncle Lionel Tracey used to say this.

I guess

Indeed; it's a fact.

"Heard you fell down the stayahs."
"I guess!"
"Did you miss a step?"
"Hell no. I hit every damn one of them."

incident at Exeter

When the UFOs landed in 1965, residents got some agitated. The landing was witnessed by many. Some sober. Some officers of the law. I b'lieve tickets were sold.

New Hampshire has hosted many UFO encounters over the years, including the abduction and subsequent probing of Betty

and Barney Hill in 1961 near Groteon. The aliens returned the
Hills to their vehicle. Betty and Barney drove home to Portsmouth,
having misplaced a few hours. They never got over it.

In 2000, a group of UFOlogists, along with Betty Hill herself,
returned to the scene of the abduction for a look-see. The gang was
standing beside the road where the UFO had landed when a local in
a pickup truck pulled over and called out, "Did ya see a moose?"

"Nope," the UFOlogists replied. "Looking for UFOs."

inebriated disk
A bad back as the result of a fall caused by imbibing

Family story: At the doctor's, my Irish grandmother was asked
if she drank. "Oh yes, every day," she said. "Tay. And water."

inneresting
*Of interest; a neutral expression that implies neither criticism nor
acclaim*

"How'd you like that new book by Dan Brown?"
"Inneresting."

jazz
Glass containers

At the village store in Franconia, a summer resident asked the
clerk for a dozen jars. She repeated her request three times, but
the clerk just looked puzzled, until finally light dawned over
Marblehead: "Oh," he said, "you mean cannin' jazz!"

jeesum or jeesumcrow
Expletive

Jennie Brown's grandmother disapproved of the use of those
words. She said, "Jennie, there are lots of good words in the

dictionary that you can use when you want to carry on." She wasn't talking about this dictionary—because it wasn't written yet.

jeesum H. bald-headed, pink-whiskered, peel-healed key-ryest

A gentle approximation of my Grampa Bill's favorite profanity

In the family story, my dad loads a green apple on the pointy end of a switch. He sees Grampa Bill away down the other end of the field, gives the switch a good snap, sending the green apple hurtling in Grampa's direction. It clonks the old man on the top of his head. A miracle hit! The last thing Dad heard before he hightailed it was, "Jeesum H. bald-headed, pink-whiskered, peel-healed key-ryest! I'm gonna kill you, boy."

jiggered

Surprised

"Paul's got a new job and it pays eleven dollars an hour to staht, plus benefits!"

"Well, I'll be jiggered!"

jimmies

Sprinkles; ants; chocolate or multicolored candies sprinkled on ice cream

The scooper at the dairy bar asked the child from away who'd ordered a large cone if he wanted jimmies.

"No," the little guy said. "I want my own."

job of work

Employment for pay

"Maxwell is forty years old and still going to school! He never had a job of work in his life."

judas priest
A cry for help

When our neighbor, Sylvester Dunn, known as Uncle Dunny, volunteered to teach me to drive, I became familiar with this expletive. Coming down Colby Hill at a good clip, my right front tire wandered onto the soft shoulder. "Judas priest," Dunny said.

junkawood
A large piece of cod wood put in the stove just before bed, so the stove will heat all night; also called a sleepa

justasoon
Rather

At the Jaffrey Historical Society meeting, the treasurer gave his report from the back of the room. The president invited him to the front, but the treasurer declined. His report was brief. He said: "We got a lot of money in. We spent a hell of a lot more. I'd justasoon not look at anybody."

just a twitch'll do 'er
Move a short distance; goes back to when hosses twitched logs out of the woods

If you're backing the car into a small space, and an observer says, "Just a twitch'll do 'er," you're almost in.

just go home
To separate from the situation in order to solve a problem

When I told a slightly off-color story at the Auburn Historical Society, I felt kinda bad. "I hope nobody's offended," I said.

Nonagenarian David Griffin piped up: "If they was, they can just go home."

kellate

Figure, calculate

"How many do you kellate will show up for the hearing?"
"The whole town and then some."

khakis

1. Tan pants

2. Instruments for starting vehicles

I heard this on National Public Radio's *Car Talk*—one of my favorite radio shows. Tom and Ray, aka Click and Clack, the hosts, speak with the quintessential Massachusetts accent, not the patrician Kennedy dialect, but the version spoken in Boston and its suburbs. Click and Clack were explaining their accent—which in this case sounds just like New Hampshire.

"Muhtha, I lost my khakis."
"How do expect to drive to work then?"
"Not my cah keys, Muhtha, my khakis. My tan pants."
"Why didn't you say so? They're in the wash."

kice

Good heavens

Bob Ramsay tells the story of Chief Barnard who got a call from the police in Concord. The police said a couple of bandits had robbed a store, stolen a car, and were headed up Hebron way. The chief was to be on the lookout. He called his deputy, Nelson Adams. They drove to the top of Hoyt Hill, where you could see most of Hebron, some of Groton, and, to the north, clear into metropolitan Plymouth.

The two men sat in the cruiser at the top of the hill into the dead of night. Finally, they spotted headlights coming fast. They knew it was the bandits. Who else would be driving through Hebron at two o'clock in the morning?

"What we gonna do now, Chief?" Nelson asked.

The chief grew thoughtful. "Kice, Nelson, if we set here quiet another five minutes, they'll be in Plymouth."

kin be

Sometimes is

> "Lottie is an awful nice person."
> "She kin be."

knock the wind out of your sails

Render breathless or speechless

At town meeting, Zeke got going on the need for an ordinance to quiet barking dogs. It turned personal when he cited the barking dogs of Amanda, the town clerk. Finally, Amanda could stand no more: "If you'd stay home nights instead of visiting the neighbor lady, you wouldn't hear my barking dogs."

That pretty much knocked the wind out of his sails.

L

laid up

So hurt or sick you can't work

When Preston broke his leg tripping over the ewe, he was laid up for six weeks. His wife felt bad.

"Preston," she said, "can I do anything for you?"

He said, "A kind word now and then would be nice."

law comes off

Open season; once the law comes off, it's legal to hunt. Hunting season ends when the law goes on.

"There was a herd of deah in my orchard every morning, eating drops, until the law come off. Then they're nowhere to be found. I think my wife tipped 'em off."

lawn awnament

Decorative object on the grass out front of the house, such as a flamingo or a big glass ball on a perch

At the church auction one of the items up for bid was a heavy-duty truck rack. The rack was not in the hall—too big—but the donor, Neil English, provided a photo and this description:

Vanguard Contractor's heavy-duty truck rack

Used one year

Bolts on to full-sized 8-foot pickup bed

70" by 100" footprint size

Was installed on a 1996 Ford F-150

Sold new for $600

Reason for selling:

My wife no longer appreciates it as a lawn awnament.

Well, Neil spelled it "ornament," but we knew what he meant.

leanin' toward Sawyer's

1. On the verge of collapse

In several towns I've been told this saying refers to the property of a family called Sawyer. In Gilford, natives take the expression to mean leaning in the direction of Sawyer's farm. The leaning implies decrepit, on the verge of collapse, as in: "That bahn with the sagging roof won't last the winter; it's leaning toward Sawyer's."

2. Sneaking out for an adult beverage

B. A. Botkin in *A Treasury of New England Folklore* says the expression refers to a person leaving the house surreptitiously or sneaking out for a drink. Seems a family named Sawyer ran a store that sold alcohol years ago in Sugar Hill.

3. Old expression related to felling trees

My friend Art Slade says the expression refers to felling trees. The sawyer notched the tree so it would fall a certain way. If it leaned the other way, in the sawyer's direction, then it was dangerous. Could be catastrophic for the sawyer. Come to think of it, didn't do the tree much good either.

leave it sit

Let alone for a while

Mix the dough then leave it sit for about four hours before you knead it again and shape it into loaves.

legislature, N.H.

The New Hampshire Legislature is the third-largest legislative body in the English-speaking world, right behind the U.S. Congress and the British Parliament.

Our House of Representatives has 400 members and the Senate has 24, despite the fact that they get paid just $100 per year plus mileage. They don't have to pay tolls and they get free parking in Concord when the legislature's in session—so they are pulling down a few bennies.

Bill Gardner, who's been New Hampshire's secretary of state since Christ wore knickers, says, "California would have to have twelve thousand members in their assembly to have the kind of per-capita representation we have in our four-hundred-plus legislature."

Yup, and everybody knows somebody, or a few somebodies, who serve in the legislature. We're not shy about letting them know what we think to help them decide how to vote. We keep track, too. Bettah b'lieve it.

let 'em don't

Let them be

On the playground, two boys had a disagreement, and a teacher wondered whether to intervene. Before she did, though, a third boy said: "Mrs. Whitcomb, if they wanna fight, let 'em fight. If they don't, let 'em don't. (Thanks to Judy Whitcomb Hall for this true story and usage.)

In a related story involving homonyms, Mrs. Whitcomb asked her students to write sentences using the vocabulary word "border." Ephraim wrote: "My mother sleeps with the border."

lieberry

A place full of books for borrowing

The English major says, "I heard of blueberries and strawberries but never lieberries."

light dawned over Marblehead

Comprehended after a period of confusion

A reference to Marblehead, Massachusetts, where, evidently, light takes a long time to dawn.

"When he got down on his knees, I thought sure he was going to propose, but then light dawned over Marblehead. He'd dropped a contact lens."

lily patch place

Outhouse, privvy, backhouse; also, necessary, ordinary

Day lilies thrive in the rich soil beside the little house with the moon on the door and along the path that leads to it.

line storm

1. Ferocious final winter storm that marks the coming of spring

Starting mid-March, optimists (like me) call every storm a line storm.

2. Storm that signals the end of fall and the beginning of winter

Optimists (like me) try to ignore that one. Hard to do, though, if it dumps a foot of snow on your roof.

littlanothin'

A cheap price

"With the bottom dropped out of the housing market, you can pick up a double-wide for a littlanothin'."

Live Free or Die

New Hampshire's die-hard motto

Coined by Revolutionary War general John Stark and featured on our license plates since 1971. Before that the plates read, simply, SCENIC. Ironically (and I remember this), folks who covered up the motto, likely in protest of the Vietnam War, got into trouble. So maybe the motto should have been, LIVE FREE BUT DON'T MESS WITH LICENSE PLATES.

A friend of mine, during that era, modified his plates to read LIVE FREE OR PIE. That didn't go over big with authorities either.

loaded for bayuh

A hunting term; put sufficient charge into the muzzleloader and you've got enough firepower to shoot a bayuh.

When a person is on a mission or a rampage, you could say, he's loaded for bayuh.

A drunk person is said to be just loaded, although a loaded person sometimes feels as though he could wrestle a bayuh.

lobstah

Ocean spider closely associated with Maine, but harvested off the coast of New Hampshire as well

The meat is so tricky to extract from the shells that restaurants provide step-by-step instructions and bibs. It's worth the trouble, though, especially when you dip the meat in melted buttah.

looking out the west window

Getting old

When Mike Cornog turned 40, young Ebenezer Tolman said, "You're looking out the west window now!"

lost my puckah string

Lacking control over one's bowels; the opposite of constipation

Jere Henley's dad commented to an old-timer that he hadn't seen him around town for a few days. The old-timer said he'd been a little under the weather.

"Oh?"

"Ayuh. I lost my puckah string."

love will go where it's sent

Just what it says; pretty romantic, right? Or not.

Marilyn Arseneau of Milford recalls her Yankee grandmother, Bertha Blodgett, using this term when she learned of the engagement of a friend to a "coarse, overbearing old coot."

"Love will go where it's sent," she said, "even if it's up a pig's ass."

lowry

Menacing

A lowry sky is gray and overcast, signaling wet weather to come. "Wanna go fishin' up Lucas Pond?"

"I dunno. That sky's looking pretty lowry, and my sciatica's kickin' up."

lug

Carry a heavy load

"Tuesday, I picked Big Ethel up at nine in the morning and lugged her all over creation."

Similar to caht, except caht implies a lighter load.

"Wednesday, I cahted Little Ethel to gymnastics and back."

lunka

A large specimen

"I thought my line was going to break for sure. That was some lunka of a rainbow."

M

maneuvr'n

Making a tricky, difficult, or clever move

"By the time Slick got through with his maneuvr'n, he owned my bamboo fly rod, and I was stuck with a bushel of cider apples and an IOU."

mawbid

Dark, twisted, relating to death or funerals; Yankees love mawbid stories.

Mabel says to Dorothy, "Are you going to Henrietta's funeral?"

"'Course not," Dorothy replies. "She wouldn't come to mine."

A woman called Dublin town hall wondering what the procedure was for purchasing a cemetery plot. "Well, I can tell you this," the clerk said. "You can't just come in cold."

Betty was very fond of her husband's parents, so naturally she attended her father-in-law's calling hours. There was her mother-in-law standing at the head of the casket. The mother-in-law says: "Betty, how do you think he looks?"

"Goo-wd," Betty says.

"What do you think of his tie?"

"Elegant," Betty says.

"I bought that tie for him three Christmases ago. He never wore it. By God, he's going to wear it now."

mawtah

Special mud used to glue bricks together

mawtified

Deeply embarassed

McMansions
Big fancy houses in developments

A development is what we call a new road or series of roads built on what used to be farmland where new houses spring up like mushrooms, and they all look more or less alike.

What do the natives have to say about McMansions?

"It's gonna cost an ahm and a leg to heat those monstrosities come winter. Hope they have deep pockets."

mebbyso
Could be true

"I heard your buddy's going to run for selectman."

"Mebbyso. Mebbynot."

Mebbynot is the opposite of mebbyso.

The shortest story I know involves a selectman. Heard it in Deering.

"Fella run for selectman once. Unopposed. And he lost."

"Was he a scissorbeak?"

"Mebbyso. Mebbynot. But he was an incumbent."

Meg Meggassen's cellar
Repository for lost objects

Nancy from Amherst said in her family, whenever something can't be located, they say, "Maybe it's in Meg Meggassen's cellah." Evidently, Meg kept quite a lot of stuff in her cellar, so it would be as good a place as any to start looking.

memba
1. One who belongs to a group

"Joann's been a memba of the Historical Society since 1945."

2. Recall

"Can't memba if I left the keys on the counter or in the bowl."

middle of the loaf

Midway through a long-term relationship

Gossip held that a certain woman was stepping out with a man who wasn't her husband. "So what," said the Yankee philosopher. "Ya never gonna miss a slice or two outta the middle of the loaf."

midgies

Tiny flying bugs; no-see-ums, but bite-ums

They slide in through the screens and eat you all over in the night. If you can't see um, you can't swat um, so you're bound to itch um.

might's well talk to a stump

Your lips are moving but nothing's getting through.

"Did you explain to Abe that he needed a permit to add an up-stayahs to his camp or else the building inspector would get after him?"

"Might's well talk to a stump. He's gonna do what he wants."

mite bit

Somewhat

John Chandler's aunt Fanny, a proper Boston lady, owned a summer home on Murray Hill in Danbury. She'd visit after mud season and stay through until fall. The first time she saw her neighbor Arthur Jewett in the spring, she politely asked, "Mr. Jewett, how have you been this past year?" (She pronounced "been" like "bean," being so very proper.)

Arthur replied, "I don't mind tellin' ya, Mrs. Reynolds, I been a mite bit constipated."

moon the Cog

A tradition among hikers on Mount Washington

Riding the Cog Railway gets people from the bottom of the mountain to the top a lot faster than anybody can hike it. The train is noisy and, until the recent conversion from coal, smoky. Hikers resent it crossing their trails and disturbing their tranquility, so when the train goes by, they moon it. Recently, law enforcement has cracked down on that practice and levied fines on the mooners.

When I rode the Cog, the conductor said that if a mooning did occur we could either avert our eyes or get out our cameras. I got out my camera.

moose

Our largest mammal; more than one moose are also moose—no such thing as mooses.

Tourists frequent Moose Alley up north, the likeliest place to spot moose. Moose tours are popular in the North Country. In fact, we have moose all over the state. With those long legs a moose can commute from Claremont to Keene in an hour. You never know where they're going to turn up.

And they're quiet. I came upon a moose in the woods behind my house. When I bent down to grab the dog by the collar so she wouldn't get into an altercation she could not win, the moose had disappeared. Silently. For a few minutes, I thought maybe I'd hallucinated it. Until I found the steaming pile of moose beans.

moose-turd pie

A North Country delicacy dating to 1800s and the lumber camps

Nobody wanted to be camp cook because the lumberjacks whined so much about their food. After a series of cooks quit in a huff, Pierre said he'd take the job temporarily. But the first person to complain would have to take over.

Meal after meal, the lumberjacks ate their beans, beef, biscuits, bacon, eggs, and potatoes without complaint. After a few weeks, Pierre got sick of being cook. Too much work. He'd rather be cutting timber than frying bacon. So he went into the woods, gathered moose turds (also called moose beans), baked them into a flaky crust, and served the pie piping hot.

Melvin took one bite: "This pie tastes like shit," he said. "But it's good."

move the question
Phrase used at town meeting to end discussion and force a vote

In Belmont, Elcid always had a lot to say at town meeting on just about any topic. Moderator Fournier enforced the rule that once you spoke on an article, you couldn't speak again until everybody else had a turn.

Elcid spoke on a budget question. Several others spoke. Elcid took his place at the back of the line to the microphone, having thought of a few other comments. He was about to step to the mic when he noticed a woman in line behind him who had not yet spoken to the question. With a gallant flourish, he said, "You go right ahead, ma'am."

She did. "Move the question," she said. And the house agreed.

Elcid was shut down on that one.

mow in the noonday sun
Do the job in the hardest way

When the carpenter was working on his house, the elderly owner took one end of the measuring tape and squatted to place it, trying to help out. He got stuck. Couldn't stand. He asked the carpenter to help him to his feet.

With tears in his eyes, the old man said: "I can't do what I used to."

The carpenter said: "Mr. Fifield, you're ninety-seven years old. You don't have to mow in the noonday sun."

muckle

Grab hold and hold tightly

"When Lizzie's feet started to slip on the wet grass, she muckled right on to me, and we both rolled down the hill."

mud season

When the snow melts and the ground gradually thaws, we call that mud season. Muddy driveways, muddy roads, muddy parking lots. Mud season anticipates blackfly season. For most of us, these are our two least-favorite seasons. Except, of course, for tax season. And winter.

Before paved roads, mud season could be even more of a challenge than it is now. During Prohibition, Terry was awakened by the revving of a touring car stuck in the mud outside his farmhouse. Four men in dark suits came to the door. "Do you have an ox to pull us out?" Coincidentally, he did. The ox did its work. The travelers were grateful and slipped him ten dollars, which was a lot of money in those days.

In the lantern light, Terry noticed several small holes in the car doors. "Are these bullet holes?" he asked.

"Yuh," the men said. "We're rumrunners. But the bullet holes aren't from the cops—they're from our competition."

Later, Terry told his friends: "I decided it would be best not to mention I was town constable."

mud worm

Small earthworm good for fishing

Cindy's father said when she was little she was fascinated by worms. One day she brought a big one to him and said, with a lisp caused by missing baby teeth, "Daddy, with ith the front and with ith the back of thith worm?"

"Why do you want to know?"

She said, "I want to kith it."

116

In Goffstown, a teller prefaced his story by saying he'd heard this from his grandfather in his formative years—when he believed everything Grampa said.

When Grampa went fishing he always took a flask of spirits, just in case. On one trip, he ran out of mud worms. Luckily, he spotted a snake on the banking of the brook. The snake had a small frog in its mouth.

Grampa took out his flask, sprinkled a few drops of spirits on the snake's mouth, and, sure enough, the snake released the frog, which Grampa put on his hook for more fishing.

A little while later, he felt a gentle poke on his ankle. It was the snake. Back with another frog.

muhtha

Married to fatha; female parent of sista and/or bruhtha

Some husbands call their wives "muhtha." I asked my friend Peg what her first husband called her. She said, "Jesusmahgret."

Mummer

What some New Hamsphire children call their mother; another example of the wandering R

mushmelon

Cantaloupe

Watermelon's good, but mushmelon's sweeter.

mushrat

Muskrat

A rodent that likes to swim—bigger than a rat, smaller than a beaver. Some people eat them. Not me.

must git

Needs to leave or suffer the consequences

This expression was unearthed from the *Franklin Transcript* of June 28, 1894, by Fred Ogmundson of North Wilmot. The names have been changed in case any relatives are still around.

The item read as follows: "Charles Jones, who has left his wife, Mrs. Lucy Messer Jones, seventeen years ago, has just returned and paid his former wife a visit. She has, during his absence, married a Mr. Pangburn. Charles has been heard to say that Lucy is as sweet and fair as ever, and Mr. Pangburn 'must git.' Wilmot people are anxiously awaiting further developments."

mux

Combines muss and mix

"Don't touch those papers. I've got 'em all in order and you'll mux 'em up."

muxed up

Scattered and confused

"It might be the new medicine or maybe a touch of Old-Timer's disease, but lately Aunt Molly's been all muxed up."

native

*Someone born in a place, who—years later—remains. Definitions
vary. Some say to be truly native you need five generations in the
ground (on at least one side of the family). Others say seven.*

When newcomers say, "I'm not a native, but my kids are," a
common response is, "Just because a cat has kittens in the oven,
don't make 'em biscuits."

One theory suggests that you become a native when the last
person dies who remembers you moving into town.

Joy raised her hand at town meeting. "Mr. Moderator, may I
speak to the issue?"

The moderator said: "How long have you lived in town?"

"Twenty-seven years," Joy said.

"All right," the moderator said, "but keep it shot."

The discussion gets tricky for folks who reside close to the
borders. For example, if you were born at a hospital in Vermont,
but your parents lived, say, in Walpole, are you a New Hampshire
native? Or a Vermont native? In 2002 (I'm not making this up),
the legislature passed a bill ensuring that in those cases, the child
would be considered a New Hampshire native.

Winston's grandparents had fourteen children. "Were they all
New Hampshire natives?" his friend asked.

"Well, there's some question about Brucie," Winston said.
"Brucie was born in Maine. But Grampa never left the state."

At The Plus-55 Club of Rye, we got talking about roots. "Who
here is a native of Rye?" I asked. Two ladies raised their hands.
One was Irene. Irene's friend said, "Put your hand down, Irene,
you're not a native."

Irene shot back, "How old do you have to be to be a native?"
Bottom line: Everybody's a native of somewhere.

The *Keene Sentinel* supposedly ran an obituary for a man born
in Chicago, who moved with his family to Keene as an infant, lived
to be 100, and was much admired for his many civic contributions—school committee, Boy Scouts, baseball coach, etc.

The headline on the obituary read: CHICAGO MAN DIES IN KEENE
HOSPITAL.

nawmul

Regular, average, as expected

A North Country banker went to a conference in Keene. After
a meeting, one of the Keene bankers said of a colleague: "That
native fella had quite an accent, didn't he?"

"Lawd no," said the North Country banker. "He was just
puttin' that on. He talks just as nawmul as you or I."

new broom sweeps clean

A person with fresh perspective can see what needs doing

In Northwood on Route 4, now called the First New
Hampshire Turnpike, up on the hill where the new Lester's
Market used to be, before it went out of business, sits a box
trailer no longer used for hauling. It's used for signage, often
political, usually pro-Republican. But when Democrat Jeanne
Shaheen ran for governor, sure enough, the trailer supported her
with the message: A NEW BROOM SWEEPS CLEAN. What the sign
maker may not have known is that this is just the first half of the
adage that ends, "but an old one knows the corners."

nightwalker

Big mud worm; doesn't walk though. No feet; more accurately called night crawlah.

A family ran a bakery and, in summer, a bait shop. One of the kids was covering the counter. The tourist asked for a dozen crullers, and got a dozen crawlahs.

nimrod

The word has biblical origins, but around here we apply it to someone who tries his or her best, but has insufficient information or is too confused to perform a task effectively.

Like when Spencer nailed his hand to the beam with the power nailer, his partner might say, "Spence, that was kind of a nimrod move," as he dials 911.

One time, up to the lake, we took the big boat out to the island. It broke down. Typical. So we were stuck—me, my husband, my daughter, her boyfriend, another friend, my brother-in-law, and mother-in-law. We had a kayak that someone had paddled out. So we came up with the bright idea of sending a volunteer back in the kayak to fetch the aluminum fishing boat, row that to the island, and evacuate some of the stranded, while others worked on the motor.

My daughter's boyfriend, whose name just happens to be Nimrod, volunteered. He paddled away in the kayak and about 45 minutes later reappeared in the fishing boat. He's a strong young man and he was rowing hard but not making a lot of progress. We watched him move up the lake in our direction, slowly.

Then I noticed my daughter, standing at the top of the ledge, yelling: "Nimrod, Nimrod, pointy end first."

I was on the couch eating my Lean Cuisine Turkey Dinner while watching *Top Chef*, when my husband, not normally a fast mover, zipped through from the garage to the bathroom. His size-13 feet were flying! "What?" I said.

He didn't have time to answer. He reappeared and slid back through to the garage with a bucket of water and a bath towel.

I followed and came upon a terrible sight.

Later, when the excitement died down, John, whose middle name happens to be Nimrod, explained what happened. He was priming clairbuds in the garage because it was nippy out and had set the gallon of white primer on a cardboard box. The box tipped. The gallon of primer launched itself—he said it "cantilevered"—and the paint went high and long, dousing his midlife crisis, a black Porsche Boxster convertible. Sponging the paint off the Porsche before it dried, seemed, to him, a matter of some urgency.

I took pictures.

nip

1. A small drink of a strong adult beverage; about ten sips constitute a nip.

2. A little bite from a little dog

Fella is sitting on a barrel in front of the general store with a dog at his feet. The tourist says, "Does your dog bite?"

"Nope," says the fella.

The tourist pets the dog on top of its pointy little head. The dog nips him. The tourist pulls his hand away, startled and kinda pissed off. "I thought you said your dog didn't bite."

Fella says, "That ain't my dog."

3. In papermaking, a dangerous place where two rolls come together; if you get a hand stuck in there, you might lose it.

Norman Greene, fifth-generation papermaker, complained to his boss at the Berlin Mills about the need for a safety guard over a nip on his machine.

"Norman," the boss scoffed, "you're a paper man! You know better than to stick your hand in an open nip."

nippy
Cool; not warm

Nippy is a relative term. A 60-degree morning in August might be called nippy. So might a 30-degree day in May. Minus-40 with a brisk wind in January, that's some nippy.

no better than he or she should be
Description of a young person who's stepped outside the bounds of what his or her elders consider proper behavior

"Is that youngest child of yours staying out of trouble?"

"He's no better than he should be. But we're hoping a stint in the army will straighten him out some. It did his brother, Hubert."

none too pleased
Unhappy

True story: Ned wanted to deepen the well so it wouldn't dry out every summer. He got ahold of some black powder. He and Junior lowered the powder to the bottom of the well in a can with a long wick attached. Ned, who's scientific, happened to think, "The force will shoot right out the top of the well."

So he and Junior and a couple other fellas hauled and levered a boulder into place to seal off the top of the well. They touched 'er off. The boulder arched into the air away up high, then fell straight through the roof of the house into the spare bedroom on the second floor.

Mrs. Ned was none too pleased.

Evidently, the boulder was too big to pass through the bedroom doorway, so there it sits, still. Ned calls it sculptcha.

nor'easter

A big storm from the Northeast, with wind and snow

When a nor'easter is forecast it's time to fill the bathtub with flushing water, button up, and hunker down.

no skin off my teeth

Doesn't trouble me

"Instead of eight, there'll be nine of us for suppah tonight."
"No skin off my teeth. We'll put another podayduh in the oven."

notch

A pass through the mountains

We have three big ones: Pinkham, Crawford, and Franconia, where the mountains seem to be coming right down on your head. Sandwich Notch is no slouch either. Even locals get a touch of the willies driving through the notches in the black of night.

not quite bright

Unintelligent

At the circus sideshow, George got to heckling the wild man from Borneo. Finally, the wild man cracked. He said, "If you kept your goddam mouth shut, folks wouldn't know you're not quite bright."

not so's you'd notice

No

> "Graham lost much weight on that noodles and pea-pod diet?"
> "Not so's you'd notice."

numb as a hake

Not bright

> A hake is a saltwater fish known for its low IQ.

numb as a pounded thumb

Thumbs aren't too sharp to begin with; pound one with a hammer and it's even number than usual.

numb as a stick

Unresponsive and unintelligent

> "I tried to tell the fella down to the TV stoah what I wanted, but he was numb as a stick, and kept tryin to sell me what I dint want. So I gave up."

nutha or whole nutha

Something else entirely

> As in: "Buying oysters by the pint, that's one thing, but raking 'em yourself and shucking 'em by hand, that's a whole nutha kettle of fish."

O

off-kiltah

1. Crooked or not sitting straight

A chair that is off-kiltah will be tippy and you might spill off it onto the floor.

2. How to describe someone with strange ideas

"Betty claims those Martian aliens were bothering 'round her place again last night, stealing chickens and digging around in the assparograss patch. She always was a little off-kiltah."

off like the maid's pajamas

Departing presently

"Soon as I get this cement poured, I'm off like the maid's pajamas to my kid's dance recital."

oh, hemlock

A polite way to say "oh, hell"

"Oh hemlock, the house's afire and I can't find my pants."

The connection between hemlock and hell also comes up in the old saying: "I want to be buried in a hemlock coffin so I can go to hell a-snappin'." When hemlock wood burns, it snaps and pops.

Old Home Day

In 1899 Governor Frank Rollins declared Old Home Week, a time for those who'd moved from their homes in New Hampshire to return.

He wrote: "Come back, come back! Do you not hear the call? What has become of the old home where you were born?" Then he went on to talk about our rolling hills, rambling farmhouses, fragrant lilacs, shimmering poplars, and weeping willows.

Many towns still celebrate Old Home Day each summer with parades, suppers, fireworks, and other exciting activities.

Old Man of the Mountain

Our state symbol, about which native son Daniel Webster famously said: "Men hang out signs indicative of their respective trades. Shoemakers hang out a gigantic shoe; jewelers a monster watch; and the dentist hangs out a gold tooth. But in the mountains of New Hampshire, God Almighty has hung out a sign to show that there He makes men."

The Old Man of the Mountain, also known as The Great Stone Face, fell off the side of his mountain in May of 2003.

We still feel pretty bad about it.

The day of the tragedy, a man and his sister were driving through the Notch. They got to the place where you could see the Old Man well, and the sister gasped: "He's gone."

The brother said, "I'm going to turn around. I've got to see that."

onaway

Anyway

At the Center Harbor Historical Society meeting, Roger welcomed visitors. "Onaway," he said, "it's good to see some strange faces."

Also pronounced *anway*.

oogle

Stare at with interest

"Al was oogling those apple pies, but Audrey said he couldn't have none onaway on account of his clestrol."

ooze

Travel without making a fuss

"What you doin' today?"

"Gonna work on Burgess's bahn in the mornin', then I thought I'd ooze over to the Dollar Store, see what's on sale; wife's birthday's coming up on Saddy."

oughtn't say that again

An apology

Wilber Cook was the plow driver in town. Storm came up, four o'clock in the morning, and he was anxious to get on the road because it was snowing like a bandit.

"Hurry up with that bacon, woman," he snapped at his wife.

Swiftly followed by, "I guess I oughtn't say that again."

outastatah

Not from New Hampshire

"Ninety-three North is jam-packed with outastatahs going skiing, so I took the back way through Bristol."

outhouse

An outdoor bathroom; also known as a backhouse or necessary

In winter, Jennie Brown reminds me, folks would bring the toilet seat indoors from the outhouse to warm it up.

In Alstead Center, the new owner of the old house hired a local builder to restore it. He said, "I want this house to be just like it was when it was first built."

The builder said, "Where do you want me to put the outhouse?"

Two brothers side by side in the two-holer, doing what needs
to be done.

Pod says, "Todd, you got a buck?"

"What do you need a buck for, Pod?"

"Just give me the buck."

Todd reaches into his overalls and hands over a buck.

Pod drops it down the hole.

"What'd you do that for, Pod?"

"I just dropped a quarter a minute ago."

"So?"

"If you think I'm crawlin' down in that hole for a quarter,
you're crazy."

Pod and Todd, when they were young fellas, thought it would
be funny to tip over the outhouse, roll it down the bankin', and
send it sailing down the Merrimack. It was funny, indeed, until
their father called them on the carpet.

"Did you boys tip over that outhouse, roll it down the bankin,
and send it sailing down the Merrimack?"

Recalling George Washington and the cherry tree, they rue-
fully admitted to having done the deed. "We cannot tell a lie,
Dad. We tipped over the outhouse, rolled it down the bankin',
and sent it sailing down the Merrimack."

Dad took Pod and Todd out behind the woodshed and administered some country discipline. "But Dad," the boys complained,
"when George Washington said he cut down the cherry tree, his
father dint punish him, because he told the truth."

"Yuh, well, George's father wa'n't in the cherry tree when
George chopped it down."

out to East Chemung and back
A trip to a remote area; also, Lost in East Chemung

Chemung is a rural section of Meredith and New Hampton. People from surrounding towns describe a long, frustrating trip as going out to East Chemung and back.

"How was the wedding?"

"Long, boring, and too fah away. By the time I got home, I felt like I'd been to East Chemung and back."

ova home
At the homestead or home place

"You oughta see the new sink Sheldon put in ova home. It's so nice I hate to dirty it."

ova to
At

"When you called I was ova to Hannafud's buying hot dogs and rolls for the barbecue."

owly
Annoyed

"Joyce was some owly when she found out Lincoln hadn't paid the electric bill. She was even owlier when the lights went out."

P

paahched
Wicked thirsty

"We ran out of water halfway through the hike up Mount Monadnock, and by the time we got back to the cah, we were paahched."

pack rat
A saver; a person who never throws anything away

In the attic, Donald Hall found a box marked STRING TOO SHORT TO BE SAVED, and used it as the title of a book of excellent essays about New Hampshire.

A woman in Pelham described her mother as a pack rat. After she died, they were cleaning out Mother's attic and found two boxes. One was marked CUPS WITHOUT HANDLES, the other, HANDLES WITHOUT CUPS.

pahtridges or pattiges
Game birds, smaller than a turkey, bigger than a woodcock

Two hunters from away walked into the shop and asked for "shot for grouse."

"What?" the storekeeper asked, stumped.

"We need shot for grouse."

Another customer translated: "Alvin, they're looking for some cahtridges for pahtridges."

Ken thinks Joe's the greatest pattige hunter in the world. They went out hunting together. Joe would hunt one side of the road and Ken the other. Ken, who has an artificial leg, can't move too fast or travel too far, hence this unusual stop-and-go hunting method.

Joe shot a pattige at the first stop. Ken was some impressed. At the next stop, Ken went his way on one side of the road. Joe took the other. Joe fired off his shotgun and hurried back to the truck. He showed Ken the dead pattige from the first stop. "Look, Ken, I got another one."

Joe pulled the same trick for four more stops and never told Ken the difference, which is why Ken thinks Joe is the greatest pattige hunter in the world.

pasturized
Healthy to drink

The visitor to the farm sat down for a glass of milk and a peanut butter sandwich. "Is this milk pasturized?" she asked.

"Oh, yes. The cows go out to pasture every day."

peak-id
Sickly and pale

"How's your sister doing since she ate those bad clams?"

"Able to be up and about and partake of nourishment, but still pretty peak-id."

pea soup
1. A thick soup made of split peas cut with broth, a staple in the North Country

Your North Country cook will prepare buckets of pea soup in the fall, leave them in the shed to freeze, then in the cold of winter cut off a slab of soup with a chain saw and warm it up in an iron skillet on the woodstove. Or, he might serve it frozen between two slices of bread: a pea soup sandwich.

Old joke: What's the difference between roast beef and pea soup? Anybody can roast beef.

2. A heavy fog that's "thick as pea soup"

Two boys from Seabrook went fishing. A fog rolled in thick as pea soup. The boys got scared—next stop Portugal? They floated around for what seemed like days. Finally, they washed up on a strange shore and spotted a native. They tried to communicate best they could: "We are from New Hampshire, U.S.A.," they said slowly and distinctly. "Do you speak English?"

"Yes," the native said.

"Where are we?" the boys asked.

"Isles of Shoals."

peel down

Remove your winter clothes for spring

Loggers were known to wear the same set of clothes all winter and then peel down in March or April and buy new.

David Howard in Walpole told about Sidney, a local character whose elderly mother had recently passed. David expressed his condolences. Sidney said: " 'Twas her own damn fault. She peeled down too early this spring."

peepas

1. Tourists who visit in the fall to admire the changing leaves

You can tell a leaf peepa by his driving—10 or 15 miles over the speed limit until he spots a bright red maple. Then he hits the brakes and peeps, or swerves onto the shoulder for picture taking.

When peepas invade, winter is right around the corner.

2. Small green frogs that peep loudly in wetlands heralding spring

When these peepas arrive, winter is truly over.

peetzer

Tomato sauce, cheese, and other delights on a circle of thin dough

In Maine, they put scallops, shrimp, and lobstah on their peetzer. We prefer pepperoni and mushrooms. That's another difference between New Hampshire and Maine.

perambulating the bounds

Walk around the ache-ridge

Technically, the selectmen of abutting towns are required by law to walk the lines between them every so often, just to make sure nothing has moved. Officials in the senior town—that is, the one that's been incorporated the longest—set the date and schedule the perambulation.

persuadah

A cat's paw; an iron bar with a "V" at the end, used to persuade nails and spikes to separate themselves from wood

"I'm trying to get this old sawhoss apart. It's rotten and needs to go on the burn pile."

"Hold on, Harold. The hammah won't do it. You need the persuadah."

phase

Used in the expression, "Don't phase him none," meaning the person is not bothered by something that might be considered bothersome

"I heard Lucky's third wife left him."

"Don't phase him none. He's used to it."

pick-id

More pointy than rounded

"Never trust a dog with a pick-ed head. They're not quite bright and apt to bite."

pickin's

Choices; often used in the phrase "slim pickin's," meaning a poor variety of choices

"If you get to the yahd sale at two in the afternoon, you'll find slim pickin's. All the good stuff goes to the early birds."

pickril

A long, slender, bony fish that hides in the weeds

Good eating if you know how to fillet them.

pick up

To clean or tidy

To say "Gotta go pick up my house before company comes" does not imply superhuman strength.

pickup

1. A truck for carrying cargo

2. A do-it-yourself supper

"Kids, I'm not cooking tonight. It's pickup."

In a pickup meal, everybody prepares their own from whatever they can scrounge in the fridge or cupboards.

pie

Our favorite dessert

My last book was called *Live Free and Eat Pie: A Storyteller's Guide to New Hampshire*. Naturally, I went around the state

135

hawking it. A fella says, "Becky Rule, I got a bone to pick with you. 'Live free or eat pie'—what kind of a choice is that?" He was kinda mad, until I explained that the title was actually *Live Free* and *Eat Pie*. Well, he says, "I can live with that."

John Scudder of Moultonborough said the Reverend Hill loved pie. So Mrs. Abel baked him his favorite, rhubarb, and instructed him to share it with his family. The pie was served after supper, but when Reverend Hill put the first forkful into his mouth, he quickly spit it out. Evidently, Mrs. Abel had substituted salt for sugar. The pie went straight into the dump.

On Sunday after church, Mrs. Abel asked the reverend how he liked the pie. He didn't want to lie or hurt her feelings, so he said, "That pie didn't last very long at our house."

pie-eyed
Having oversized eyes caused by too much liquor

The Union soldier got pie-eyed and strayed from camp. Next morning, he returned, two captive Rebel soldiers tied on the back of a horse. His comrades were amazed: "How'd you catch 'em, Les?"

"I surrounded 'em."

pike
1. A busy road

" 'Steada taking the back way like usual, we took the pike. Big mistake. The traffic was solid."

Overheard in Greenland at an intersection:
"How far to the pike?"
"Fifteen minutes if you take the road to the right."

"What if I go straight?"

"You'll be swimming."

2. A big toothy fish

Hugh and his son went fishing in Skatutakee Lake. The boy hooked a two-foot pike, netted him, and flopped him into the boat. "What do I do now, Dad?"

"Grab him by the eyes." Hugh's boy grabbed the fish by the eyes. "Now what?"

"Don't know. Never caught one of those before."

pinched

Caught doing something wrong

A lawbreaker gets pinched by a police officer or game warden. He might be given a ticket for speeding or get his fishing permit taken away for having too many trout in his kreel. Nobody likes getting pinched.

At the Squam Lakes Association annual pancake breakfast, we swapped fishing stories, some fishier than others. Bob's brother-in-law, from Massachusetts, tossed a line into a brook and caught a few square-tails. Along comes the warden, who asks to see a license. The brother-in-law, just visiting New Hampshire for a couple days, has no license. To avoid getting pinched, he says, "I didn't catch these fish out of this brook. These are my pet trained fish."

The warden says, "What?"

"I put them in the brook, and when I call them they come back. I've trained them to do this."

The warden expresses a degree of disbelief.

The brother-in-law says, "I'll show you," and proceeds to dump the fish in the brook. Time passes. After a while the warden says, "So when do the fish come back?"

The brother-in-law says, "What fish?"

pipes catch

During a cold snap, your pipes might catch—get plugged with ice—especially if they're not insulated properly

Best to leave a faucet dripping and the cupboard doors open. Even then, in a real hard freeze, just about everybody will have a pipe or two catch or seize up. If the freeze goes on too long, pipes will burst. It's a pain, but we're used to it.

pissa

Of high quality

"Bob Young's blue Corvair is a real pissa."

It can also be used sarcastically, as in: "How do you like my new hat?"

"It's a pissa."

The complete expression goes, "I hope that hat is waterproof, because it's a pissa."

piss hole in the snow

Something inconsequential, neither lasting nor significant; best ignored

"All that lawyah talk don't amount to a piss hole in the snow."

piss-poor

Not up to snuff

A carpenter can lay a piss-poor roof that leaks in the next rainstorm. A mason can build a piss-poor chimbley that leans toward Sawyer's. Some say tofu makes a piss-poor substitute for chicken, but others find it delicious.

pistol

A sharp, spunky character like my friend Jean Lane of Northwood

When Jean's car slid off the road into a watery ditch during a terrific rainstorm, the emergency crew offered to help her climb out. "No," she said. "I'll sit right here. I'm going down with my ship."

Likely the phrase relates less to small firearms and more to the expression "full of piss and vinegar."

Jo Fearon of Bedford is a pistol. I met her when she was 92. She told the harrowing tale of a year or two back when she fell in her garage and broke her femur. It was a chilly day. The garage door was open. The cement floor was damp. She couldn't move even to crawl up the three steps to the kitchen door and try to phone the rescue squad. "I sat on that floor for five hours," Jo said. "Three cars went by. They waved."

Finally, a garbage truck pulled into the driveway. The driver noticed something wrong. "He swooped in and rescued me." She said. "I always wished to be picked up by a handsome young man in uniform. Guess I should have been more specific."

The day after I turned 50, I was telling stories at the Pleasant View Retirement Home. My birthday was on my mind, so I blurted it out. "I turned fifty yesterday." I could see they weren't impressed. So, thinking quick, I said: "I guess I'm about halfway there."

A lady in the audience said, "I'm ninety-nine. I guess I'm 'bout all the way there."

What a pistol.

pitcha

1. A baseball player who throws from the mound

"Pedro Martinez was a real good pitcha when he played for the Red Sox."

2. A photograph

"I hate having my pitcha taken, so put that damn camera away!"

3. A jug or a container for liquid, like lemonade: "Pour me a swig from that pitcha, would you? I'm paahched."

Joann Bailey, in her history of Northwood, tells of a boy who was given a pitcha and sent to the well to draw water for his mother, a "demanding, nagging woman." At the well, the boy decided he'd had enough of nagging. He set the pitcha "on the well curb" and walked down the road.

"Twenty years passed," Joann writes. "Some who tell the story say nearer thirty." A handsome, well-dressed stranger was observed filling a pitcha at the pump. He proceeded to walk into the house and hand it to his aged mother.

Pledge, The

To get elected to state office in New Hampshire, politicians of all parties take The Pledge, promising that they will not vote to institute any broad-based taxes such as income or sales tax.

Politicians who don't take The Pledge usually lose. Some say, when those who take The Pledge win, the state loses. It's controversial.

podayduh

Starchy root vegetable; also pronounced potatuh

Frank was out digging podayduhs in his patch. His neighbor Tom came along. "Those podayduhs ain't very big, Frank."

Frank said, "I grow them to fill my mouth, not yours."

poim or pome

Verse; someone who writes poims is a poit.

Several years ago, I led a writing workshop at the historical society in Stratford. We were about to begin when I noticed a man standing at the back of the hall. A woman in front motioned to him: "Come on in," she said. "You're not late. We're just gettin' stahted."

We got started. We wrote, read, discussed. After about an hour, I called a halt. "We'll take a short break," I said. "But come right back. We've got another hour to go."

The latecomer stood up directly in front of me, and I could tell by the look in his eyes that he was about to make a break for it.

I said, "You are coming back after the break, aren't you?"

He said, "I ain't a poit nor a writer. I just stopped by to fix the furnace."

poke

Considerable distance

It's quite a poke from Keene to Pittsburg—almost 200 miles, all tolled.

polecat

Skunk

People from away sometimes think a polecat under the porch is a kitty and try to coax it out. This is a mistake.

Frank Eastman of Chatham used to say: "I'd rather eat a skunk's ass than a tomato." Evidently he didn't care for tomatoes.

popple

Poplar; quaking aspen; the wood of the popple tree gives off very little heat when it burns.

"We nicknamed the new neighbor Popple because he worked up a big old popple tree for firewood, thinking it would keep him wahm all winter. It dint."

potluck

A meal in which everybody brings something to share, usually a casserole involving macaroni and tuna, or chicken; sometimes meatballs; I usually bring a pasta salad.

One time in college we held a potluck and everybody brought cheese and crackers—that was disappointing. Church and historical society potlucks, however, are usually a gourmand's delight. (*Gourmand* is French for somebody who likes to put on the feed bag.) The key is to be first in line for best pickin's. Those at the end of the line may find slim pickin's. Once at a sports dinner at the high school, I ended up at the end of the line, and the only thing left was a spoonful of dried-up macaroni and cheese.

pound sand

A simple but useless activity

If you tell somebody to "go pound sand," you're telling them to go away and do something that won't amount to a hill of beans. It's an insult. If you say someone "doesn't know enough to pound sand," you're suggesting they're not quite bright.

po-utch

A verandah

Some po-utches are screened in, some are open-air. The stereotype is that New Englanders spend a lot of time in rocking chairs on their po-utches. Not likely. Too much work to do, like stocking up on cod wood for the long wintah.

They tell about the Northumberland farmer renowned for drinking a lot of coffee. This was back in the '50s when Chase & Sanborn was real popular. Somehow the Chase & Sanborn people got wind of this farmer and his love of coffee, so they sent a publicity fella out to the farm to interview him for a radio ad.

Sitting on the po-utch the publicity fella began by asking the farmer how much coffee he drank.

"Quite a lot," the farmer said.

"Five cups a day?"

"Mor'n that."

"Ten cups a day?"

"Mor'n that."

"Fifteen cups a day?"

"Sounds about right."

"Good lord," the publicity fella said. "Doesn't that keep you awake?"

"Well," the farmer said, "it helps."

Seabrook Pete was standing on a po-utch one morning early, visiting with his buddy Warren.

"Pete," Warren said, "would you have a cup of coffee?"

Pete said, "Don't mind if I do."

After a while, noting the empty cup, Warren said, "Pete, would you like another cup?"

"Why, yes," Pete said, "I could use a little more."

After a while Pete's cup was once again empty. "Pete, could you use a refill?"

Pete said, "I could."

Warren said, "Pete, you must really like coffee."

Pete said, "I do. That's why I drink so much hot water, just to get a little of it."

poutine
French fries with gravy

This is a French-Canadian delicacy, available at restaurants in the North Country. Sometimes called heart attack on a plate, but always tasty.

Presidential Range
Some of our grandest mountains are named for U.S. presidents: Washington, Adams, Jefferson, Madison, Eisenhower, Pierce, and Monroe.

We also have Mount Clinton, but it's not named for Bill.

prickabush
Raspberries, blackberries, or other thorny plants

"The bear chased me through the woods, and I run smack into the prickabush. Look at my arms, all tore up from the thons."

professional liar
Storyteller, like me

At the Nottingham senior picnic, a stranger asked what I did for work. I said, "I'm a professional liar."

He said: "Are you in the House or the Senate?"

puckabrush

Thick bushes

"I chased the bear down the road but he disappeared into the puckabrush." Puckabrush may include patches of prickabush.

punkins

Large orange squash

The Keene Punkinfest, held each October, is so well attended it stops traffic downtown. For a while, Keene held the world's record for most jack-o'-lanterns in one place at one time, 29,762.

punkinseeds

Kibbies; sunfish; little fish that hang around docks and aren't very good to eat

"What's biting today, Tom?"
"Nothing but black flies and punkinseeds."

purchase

A hold, grip, or leverage

Buddy says: "I may not outlive this rock, and I can't outmuscle it, but I'm pretty sure I can out outsmaht it."
"That right, Bud?"
"Yup. One more purchase with the crowbar and, she don't know it yet, but she'll move."

put it in the basket

Throw it away

Caught chewing gum in school, you were told to put it in the basket, which meant throw the gum away.

put on the feedbag

Prepare for a meal

"Saw Rolly heading over to Erma's house about five o'clock. Second time this week he put on the feedbag with Erma."

"Romance brewing?"

"Wunt be surprised."

puttery

Complicated and time-consuming

Making tabouli from scratch is puttery. You have to chop the mint, garlic, tomatoes, and cukes; squeeze the lemons; and soak the bulgur before you can mix it all up.

My brother says tabouli tastes like bear puke. I say, "How do you know?"

Q and R

quat

A unit of measure: four quats make a gallon; two pints make a quat.

"I'd like to buy a pint of scallops."

"Don't sell 'em by the pint. Sell 'em by the quat."

"I'll take half a quat."

Clyde told Francis about the disaster at the hardware store. A shelf that held paint collapsed. The cans fell, tops popped off, and it was a big wet mess.

Francis said: "Gorry, Clyde. Must have been a nightmare—all those gallons and gallons of paint spilt on the floah in the stoah!"

Clyde said: " 'Twas mostly quats."

quicker than three shakes of a lamb's twitchet

Fast

rack

Set of antlers

"You shoulda seen the rack on that buck. Twelve points at least."

"Whyn't you shoot it?"

"Um . . . gun jammed. Sun in my eyes. Tree in the line of fire. And, too small, too fah away."

rammin' the roads

Traveling hard, as in fighting thick traffic down Nashua way, or bouncing over rough roads made rougher by mud season or frost heaves

"Dentist appointment, shopping, visited Morrie out in East Podunk. Spent most the afternoon and half the evening rammin' the roads."

rayshosses

Resources

At a meeting in Seabrook, a woman got herself worked into a tizzy over how Americans are wasting natural resources.

Wingate, arriving late, caught just the end of her rant. "Them national rayshosses ain't wasted," he said. "Far as I know, they turn 'em into glue."

relations

Relatives

"She gave a party and invited all the relations, even distant cousins."

"Those are the best kind."

Or:

"Loretta's so proud of having John Stark as a distant relation. Every time she meets somebody, within five minutes, the general comes up in conversation."

"You know what Aunt Florence always said—people who brag about their dead relations are like podayduhs—all the best parts are buried."

reputtin'

Repeat putting

Cheryl Johnson of Plymouth offers this useful word for our linguistic pleasure. "Yesterday, March 27," she wrote, "the temperature was in the fifties. The sun was out and spring was clearly here, so my husband—a seventh-generation New Hampshire man—decided to forego wearing his long underwear for the first time since last November. Today dawned gray, wet, and spitting snow. He looked out the window, turned back to the bedroom, saying he was 'reputtin' on his long johns.' "

No sense peeling down too soon. Might catch the epizudic.

rescue burro

Helpful animal

Burros used to be used to rescue hikers in the White Mountains before snow machines, ATVs, and helicopters.

Once in a while a burro would escape its pen and go hiking on its own. One unlucky burro slipped over a cliff and fell to his death. After a few days, its cahkiss started to smell and the stench disturbed hikers on the trail above. According to local legend, Joe Dodge set out to solve the problem. He used ropes to lower himself down to the spot where the cahkiss lay and went to work with a shovel.

A couple of hikers, passing by, heard him digging down below. They leaned out over the cliff and hollered down, "What you doing?"

Joe yelled back, "Digging a hole for my ass."

reverent

Preacher

Latecomer to church whispers to her neighbor: "Oh deah, I've missed half the service. What's the reverent talkin' about?"

"Ain't said yet."

riggin'

Unusual character, someone who misbehaves but nothing serious; often used in the expression:"What a riggin'."

"The next thing I know, Martha's at the top of the ladder. I said, 'Get down from there!' She's ninety, you know. I said, 'What on earth were you doing up there?' 'Takin' in the view,' she says. What a riggin'!"

right side of the grass

Alive

"How you doing?"

"All right, I guess. At least I'm on the right side of the grass."

ril

Genuinely; very

"She's ril upset. Who wouldn't be? If somebody stole my pocketbook right outta my shopping caht, I'd be some perturbed, too."

river driver

A logger who specializes in guiding the logs downriver from the forests where they were felled to the mill where they're made into paper

To avoid a fight with a river driver, never touch his cant dog, pick pole, or picaroon—the tools of the trade.

roadkill

Dead animals hit by cars lying in the road or by side of the road

In Hollis, the husband hit a deer and killed it, with considerable damage to the vehicle.

The wife says, "If you'd been going the speed limit, you wouldn't have hit it."

He says, "If I'd been going faster, I wouldn't have hit it either."

room to sulk

Adequate space

"How much land you get with your new house?"

"Twenty-three acres plus or minus. Just about enough room to sulk."

rubbahing

Listening in on the party line

Similar to rubbah neckin', or going to extremes to satisfy your curiosity. If you see a crash by the side of the road, you turn your neck all which ways to get a look at the damage. A neck made of rubbah would be handy for this.

At the Robert Frost farm in Derry, they say that Robert Frost liked to listen in on his neighbors' phone conversations. Being from California but known as a New England poet, he didn't call it rubbahing; he called it research.

ruckus
Free-for-all, melee, small riot

Dave from Marlow recalls the night Gramps fell in the outhouse pit at camp. Seems that in the spring of the year somebody dug a new pit and moved the outhouse, as it is wise to do every few years to avoid buildup. Gramps didn't get the memo about the move.

Nature called in the middle of the night. Gramps shuffled to the outhouse. That is, he shuffled to the place where the outhouse used to be, fell in the old pit, and hollered bloody murder.

Thinking quick, the boys pulled Gramps from the pit and tossed him off the end of the dock. It was April. He hollered more bloody murder.

But that wasn't the ruckus.

The ruckus came later. The neighbors, hearing Gramps hollering, called the police, who arrived shortly thereafter, with sirens, blue lights, and a fire truck for good measure.

rud
Road

Visitors asked the storekeeper how to get to the Maplewood Cemetery. Evidently they were looking up some dead relations. The storekeeper said (this is how they heard what they thought he said), "Drive up this rud, three or four miles, 'til you come to the hill and you see the Todd Rud goes off to the left. Drive about a half-mile up the Todd Rud and you'll see the gate to the cemetery. Can't miss it."

The visitors drove three miles, four miles, five miles—and back—but never saw a sign for the Todd Road. They returned to the store, agitated. After considerable back-and-forth, they figured out that the unmarked road to which the storekeeper referred was not the Todd Road, but the tarred road. After that, they found the cemetery they sought in three shakes of a lamb's twitchet.

rugged

Strong; applies to muscles as well as odors

"Henrick, he was rugged. Tucked a fifty-pound sack of flour under each arm and waltzed up Beezley Hill like it was nothin'."

Or:

"I wouldn't let Dusty into the house after his encounter with the skunk."

"Stink?"

"I guess! It was some rugged."

S

sammin eggs

Red globules used as bait for fishing even in lakes and ponds where there are no sammin

On Highland Lake in East Andover—where there are no sammin, but plenty of trout, pickril, and pout—outastatahs were trying their luck. They sat in their boat catching nothing, while, no more than 100 feet away, Brigham Doyle was hauling fish in one after another. The visitors tried worms and sammin eggs. They cast dry flies and wet. They pulled out every lure in their tackle boxes. No luck. Not even a nibble.

Finally, in frustration, one called out to Brig: "How come you're catching fish, and we're not?"

Brig said: "I'm a native."

sammin wiggle

Canned salmon and peas in a white sauce over toast

"When company came unexpected and stayed for suppah, us kids knew it would be either waffles or sammin wiggle."

sardine act

Cram a lot of people into a small space: A family of four squished into the cab of a truck—that's the sardine act.

"Are we taking the pickup or the Buick today?"

"We're doing the sardine act."

sass

Fruit sauce

Old-time cooks made rhubarb sass, blueberry sass, strawberry sass, but the all-time favorite was good old-fashioned apple sass.

scarce as hen's teeth

Rare

Hens have no teeth. Neither do roosters—but they can sure do a job on you with those beaks.

scissorbeak

Our friend Dick Hardy used this term, may even have coined it. A scissorbeak is a flatlander with an attitude of superiority or entitlement. We consider them odd birds.

"Did you enjoy your trip to the outlets?"

"No. It was wall-to-wall scissorbeaks, pushing and shoving, and spending money like it was watah. I got in line to buy a pair of steel-toed boots, and this beak cuts right in front of me like I was invisible. I dunno, maybe I am."

scoach

A little bit

"Would you slide over just a scoach so Jasper can sit on the bench, too?"

scooch

1. To crouch

"That brat scooched down in a dark corner, jumped up, and yelled, 'Boo.' I 'bout jumped out of my skin."

2. To slide along on your butt

One fella tells this sad story: "I scooched down the ledge, but met a rock staying in place while I continued on south. Left the seat of my pants on Mount Jefferson."

scotch

If you leave a hot iron on a cotton shirt too long, it'll scotch.

seagulls are walking

Foggy

New Hampshire has just 18 miles of coast, but a lot is packed into those miles, including Hampton Beach, Rye Beach, Odiorne Park, and Wallis Sands. When the fog gets extra thick, traffic slows. Even the seagulls are walking.

season

To let something or someone be for a couplethree seasons at least; let it age

When Mike Faiella bought land in Farmington in the late '70s, his nearest neighbor, Elmer Thompson, explained the standoffishness of another neighbor. He said, "Around heah we like to season a man."

see ya made it

A friendly greeting

Agnes hadn't seen her sister in 35 years since the sister moved to Florida. She traveled the 1,500 miles to Jacksonville for the reunion. She walked up to the house and knocked, having bridged those many years and miles.

Her sister stood behind the screen door, hands on hips.

"See ya made it," she said.

selectmen

Elected officials who look after the business of the town; small towns elect three, larger towns five.

The job of selectman is generally throught to be thankless and miserable, although some seem to really enjoy it.

In different parts of the state, the word is pronounced differently. Some say *se-LECT-men*. Some say *SEE-lec-men*. In New Hampton, they say *slickmen*. That's my favorite.

sexton

The person appointed to care for cemeteries

At town meeting in Brookline almost every year somebody new in town would ask about the money in the budget allotted for the sexton. "What's a sexton?" the newcomer would ask.

Grover Farwell would reply: "I'm the sexton. And I'm goin' to bury you."

Mary Stuart of Warner told of being brand-new in town and walking over to visit her neighbor at the next farm. She knocked on the door, and a voice said: "Come on in. You don't have to knock in the country." Elsie Rufe, the neighbor, was most welcoming. The women had a pleasant visit. "I'm sorry you didn't meet my husband, Gus," Elsie told Mary. "He's down in the cemetery." Oh, Mary thought, that's sad.

The next week, Mary visited again, and this time she took Elsie at her word and didn't bother to knock. She found Elsie in the kitchen candling and cleaning eggs. Again, a nice visit. Again, Elsie told Mary as she got up to leave, "I'm sorry you didn't meet my husband, Gus. He's down in the cemetery." Which Mary thought a little strange, Elsie repeating herself that way. But sometimes older people do repeat themselves.

On the third visit, Mary walked straight through the door. No Elsie, but a man sat at the table. Big as life. "Hello," he said. "I'm Gus."

Mary didn't faint away, but pretty near.

Later, she learned that Gus Rufe was the sexton.

Shaker your plates

Clean your dishes

The Shakers, a religious group with settlements in Canterbury and Enfield, were known for their tidiness as well as their clever inventions, including the flat (as opposed to round) broom. After supper, good housekeepers Shaker their plates, dry them, and put them neatly away in the cupboard.

Also, around here, Shaker is synonymous for high quality. When you Shaker a basket of berries, you guarantee that the berries at the bottom of the basket are just as good as the ones on top.

shake the dew off the lily

Visit the men's room

Recalled by Loisanne Foster as something an elderly friend would say of her husband: "Oh, George has gone to shake the dew off his lily."

shit a clinker

Be astonished

In coal-fired boilers on trains, a clinker was the rock-hard detritus left when the coal burned away. It clinked in the chamber.

When Ola Oleson was a toddler, his father, Alden, would carry him on his back as he walked the north woods, spotting trees to be cut for the logging business. Back then, the logs were twitched out with huge work hosses.

Ola said: "I crawled under one of those big work horses and was petting him under his belly. When my old man saw that, he almost shit a clinker."

shock

A stroke

"Uncle Val couldn't move the right side of his body on account of he had a shock."

shoe-uh
Certain

"Ah you shoe-uh you want coffee in your shredded wheat, Ruth?"

"I'm shoe-uh," the little girl said, "That's how Grampa likes it."

Grampa had a touch of palsy, so as he drank his morning coffee he'd get to shaking and some would spill into his cereal. Mom didn't want to embarrass Grampa, so what could she say, but okay?

Decades later Ruth says: "Coffee in shredded wheat? Oh, it's delicious."

shot

1. The new funeral director was surprised to hear the selectman was shot.

"Gosh, Wally," he said, "you'd think I'd be one of the first to hear about the selectman being shot, since I'm the only funeral director in town."

"I didn't say he was shot," Wally shot back. "I said he was shot. Not very tall."

2. Of brief duration

In Freedom, they said: "Town meeting should be shot this year. Betty Goodnow is in Florida."

3. You can take a shot with a gun.

4. You can drink a shot of whiskey.

Best not to take a shot after you've had a shot, no matter what you've got a bead on.

shots
1. Cut-off pants worn during hot weather

In November, the wise guy who owns Clark's Hardware put this message on the sign out front: PROBABLY SAFE TO PUT AWAY THE SHOTS.

2. Underpants

Albert Longly, at New London Hospital, told a volunteer he couldn't be discharged yet because he was waiting for his shots. She said, "Shall I check with the nurse?"

"No," he said. "Check with the laundry."

shuggah
Used instead of a swearword to express dismay

If you've made bread from scratch, and it's rising nicely in pans on the table under a dish towel, and then your cat jumps up and flattens the rising dough, you might say, "Shuggah!"

That's not what I said when it happened to me, though.

Variation: "Shuggah rhuggah!" My friend Ada Hatch often says this during rip-roaring card games of Nine Hands or Oh Hell. It's the equivalent of "Gosh darn it all to heck."

shunt wonder
Expect; wouldn't be surprised

"Do you think she and him will get married?"

"Shunt wonder. They've been going together for nineteen years. And her muhtha wants things made right."

sick a-bed in the wood box
Very ill

Jennie Brown of Gorham says: "As children, ill with fever, we were said to be sick a-bed in the wood box. This came from the literal, as I remember at least once being bedded down in the wood box, which, of course, was near the stove, and, thus, the warmest place in the house. Was at the doctor once, he asked how I was doing, and when I said sick a-bed in the wood box, he had no idea what I was talking about."

He must have been a flatlander.

sidehill wampus

Cousin to Bigfoot but with one leg shorter than the other, for easier travel around the slopes of steep hills

Helpful hint: To escape the sidehill wampus, head down the hill to the flat where you can likely outrun him.

sidewards

Neither forward nor backward

The fella from Greenland, having not much money for groceries, ate mostly crab he caught himself. He said, "I've et so much crab lately I'm walking sidewards."

since Christ wore knickers

Describes the passage of a long period of time

"I haven't danced a foxtrot since Christ wore knickers."
Variation: Since Moses wore knickers.

since Hector was a pup

Several years

"Haven't seen Billy around town since Hector was a pup."
"That's because he moved to Florida."

sista

Sibling to bruhtha; daughter to a muhtha and fatha

Plumber Jed got called to the new guy's house to fix a clogged sink. The new guy had lived in town only six or seven years, but he knew to call Jed Johnson for his plumbing needs. Jed was the best plumber in the area, and charged fair prices, too.

Jed was under the sink working away, when the new guy got a phone call from the tax collector, a woman who took her job seriously and had done so for 50 years, give or take. Evidently, the new guy had made a mistake and bounced his check for property taxes. The tax collector was irate. She reamed him out.

After the newcomer hung up the phone, his left ear ringing, he said out loud, "That Shirley Dow, she's a real witch." Only he didn't say witch.

Jed came out from under the sink. "Ayuh," he said. "That's my sista."

New Hampshire is a small state. Many of us are related. So be careful what you say and to whom.

sit up and take notice
Pay attention

"Didn't really want to paht with that bird dog, but when that young fella from Candia offered me a hundred dollars, cash, well, that made me sit up and take notice."

skeet
Clay disk used for target practice

The newlywed tried his wife's home-baked cookies. "Do you like them, honey?" she asked.

"Make good skeet."

skivvies
Underpants

Ezra was known to be warm-blooded—that is, the cold didn't phase him much. On days when it was some nippy, 20, 30 below, Ezra was known to set out on his porch in his skivvies, taking some sun.

"Is that right?" I asked his neighbor.

"Ayuh," the neighbor said. "Wa'n't pretty."

skun

Past tense of "skin"

Leslie fell off her bike and skun her knee.

That romantic fella Claude skun the roadkill raccoon. Then he stretched and tanned the pelt to make a hat for his fiancée.

skunked

1. To lose a game without scoring

"Losing to Belmont sixteen zip was ignominious. We got skunked."

2. To be unsuccessful

"I went into town to get my hair cut and buy a bilge pump. The hairdresser was closed and Bickford's was fresh out of pumps. I got skunked."

slick as a bean

Smooth

A government that worked efficiently would be said to run slick as a bean. Should such a thing ever happen.

slick as a gig

Smooth; usually refers to something mechanical

"How's that 'lectric winch working for you?"
"Slick as a gig."

slower'n molasses runnin' uphill in January

Very slow

"Been waitin' for my tax rebate since April. That friggin IRS—slower'n molasses runnin' uphill in January!"

smaht

Bright, intelligent, clever, quick

> "That Justice David Souter from Weare, he's ril smaht."

smahts

1. Painful

> "I stepped on a nail in my stockin' feet and it really smahts."

2. Brains

> "That lawyer's got a lot of smahts."
> "He thinks he does."

smelt'n

The scooping of small fish with big nets, generally done in the dead of the night by lantern light; smelt run in the dead of night, even though they have no legs.

Often smelt fishers require some lubrication with adult beverages to ward off the chill. Lisa Rollins from Ashland passed on this true story:

"About thirty-five years ago or so, my father Ben Rollins, along with his best buddy Kent Smith Sr. (God rest his soul), and a few other buds were out late one night smelt'n. Each man carried his smelt dipp'n net, pail, and lantern. Dad was a pipe smoker. He always smoked George Washington tobacco, and, on special occasions, Half & Half tobacco.

"As they were walking down a path next to a stream running into Big Squam, each man stepped over a low-lying wire fence. This fence was right at the end of the dock where they would wait for the smelt to run. As they stepped over the fence, each called out to the guy behind to 'watch out for the fence.'

"Apparently, Dad didn't hear the guy in front of him. He fell ass over teakettle into the drink along with the net, pail, lantern, and pipe. He went straight to the bottom, then popped back up like a cork with the net, pail, and lantern in his hands. The lantern was still lit and his pipe was still clenched between his teeth! After fishing him out of the drink, the boys rushed him home for a change of clothes and a couple shots of whiskey.

Later they went back to the smelt'n spot, scooped up a nice mess of smelts, and brought 'em home to fry. Ain't nothing tastes much better than freshly caught smelts about one o'clock in the morning."

smidge

More than a pinch, less than a scoach

smush

1. Flatten

"Georgia sat on Uncle Harvey's hat. Smushed it."

2. Mush together

"First you simmer the apples 'til they're soft. Then you smush them with sugar and cinnamon."

snap

A last-minute hash dish for supper

Arthur Slade, whose family ran inns, explains: "In my mother's parents' home, snap could have been just about anything that my grandmother could lay her hands on, generally a hash of some nature. My father was an experienced cook and he could not believe how she could take different foodstuffs and still create the same item. She could be expecting six for supper and twenty-six arrive. No problem; she would still serve on time and as planned."

snappy old cheese

Extra tasty, well-aged cheese

Snappy old cheese makes a man sit up and take notice.

snew

Past tense of snow

> "Get out the shovel and prepare to dig. It snew all night."

snot

1. A small drink

> "How about a drink?"
> "I'm due home."
> "Just a snot."
> "Well, p'rhaps, just one."

2. A person with a stuck-up attitude

When Ben was a kid he had a pet chicken named Lucy who liked to lay eggs on the guest-room pillow. Uncle Ed arrived for a visit just as Lucy was announcing she'd laid another egg. Ed was kind of a snot. When he found out what Lucy had done, he said, "I will not stay in this house!" And he never visited again.

snowing like a bandit

Snow coming down hard and fast; small flakes are the worst kind, because you know the storm's going to last a while and the snow's going to accumulate.

In Woodstock one year the road agent suggested the town invest in a new snowplow.

A fella concerned about taxes said, "They're buying a new snowplow in Lincoln. Maybe we could go in halves with them and share the machine."

The road agent said, "In my experience, when it's snowing in Lincoln, it's snowing in Woodstock."

snow machine

Snowmobile; sled; Ski-Doo

At water rides, people try to fly their snow machines from good ice to good ice, or from grass to gravel over open water. Not the brightest move, but entertaining for onlookers.

snow roller

In olden times, horses pulled snow rollers up and down the roads to compact the snow for travel by sleigh.

Our family story goes like this: When they were young, Uncle L. E. Ford and my grandfather-to-be Bob Stewart attended a card party at the homestead on top of Ford Hill. When it was time for Bob to go home, L. E. offered to ski him down the road, which had been nicely rolled after the storm. They had just the one pair of skis— those long wooden ones with the leather straps. L. E. strapped himself on and directed Bob to stand on the skis behind him.

L. E. had the poles. As luck would have it, the back-and-forth travel of sleighs over the rolled snow had left convenient ruts about two feet apart. With the skis in the ruts, L. E. wouldn't even have to steer.

L. E. lit his pipe, stuck it in his mouth, and they struck off, Bob holding on to L. E.'s waist for dear life, leaning into the turns when L. E. said lean. It was dark out, but there was a full moon. They got going down the steep part of Ford Hill when L. E. spotted something dark in the distance. Something dark and flat and evidently filling their left rut. It was a frozen horse flap.

L. E. yelled to Bob, "We're going to have to lift our left feet," as they bore down on the blockage.

They did.

But in the process lost their balance and went ass over teakettle.

It was quite a tumble. When they came to, L. E.'s first words were, "Bob, I've lost my pipe."

Grammie Ford found the pipe the following spring, picking strawberries. So that was lucky.

so don't I

Me, too; also, so don't you, so don't she, so don't he, and so don't Bobby

"Genevieve's got a bad case of poison ivy."

"So don't Bobby, and so don't I."

some

Very, or extra

"That fudge was some sweet. Made my teeth ache."

son of a biscuit

Expletive

When Jean ran the needle of the treadle sewing machine over her finger, she said, "Son of a biscuit!" Then she bled on the quilt.

soupy

Gardens in mud season; too thin to plow, too thick to drink

sozzle

Wash by hand

Loisanne Foster picked this up from her elders when she was a child. "I'm going to sozzle some clothes."

Nowadays, Loisanne gets blank looks from folks when she uses expressions like this, but that doesn't stop her.

spaghetti suppah

Usually held as a fund-raiser for a nonprofit group

Angela, new in town, volunteered to shop for the spaghetti suppah. "Shall I get tomatoes, oregano, garlic?"

"Oh no," said the veteran cooks. "We don't need any of that."

"Well," said Angela, "what will we use for sauce?"

"We've got a case of tomato soup."

That's not so bad. A certain relative of mine said his wife's idea of an Italian dish was ketchup on noodles.

spell

1. A moment of weakness or illness; dizziness

"We called 911 because Jeremy was having a spell. His eyes rolled back in his head and we couldn't get him to wake up. The EMTs came quick though, and jump-stahted him. He's doing fine now."

2. Also, to take over for someone for a short time

"You been painting that bahn for hours. Why don't I spell ya? Go get a drink of cold water or something. You're looking kinda peak-id. Next thing I know you'll be having a spell."

3. Also, a short period of time

"I could spell you for a spell, if you want."

spider

Cast-iron fry pan, which in the days of fireplace cooking had little feet

"Nothin' tastes like bacon fried up in a spider."

"Those no-stick-um pans? I wouldn't give 'em house room."

spleeny

1. Weak, unworthy

"Those goddamredsox woulda won if they weren't so spleeny."

2. Also, squeamish or chicken

"I'm kinda spleeny about going to the dentist."

spruced up

Cleaned up, polished

> "Reverent Tirabassi's comin' to suppah."
> "We better get spruced up, and the house, too."

sputterin'

Lodging a series of complaints in rapid succession

> "Russ went into the meetin' in a good mood, but he come out just a sputterin'."

staht

Get going

> "What do you folks in New Hampshire do all winter?"
> "Mostly we staht cahs."

stayahs

Steps from one level to another

> "Those stayahs are awful steep and narrow. Gram has trouble maneuvr'n 'em with her walka."

'steada

Abbreviation for instead of; a substitution

> "He accidentally delivered the five yards of gravel to Moe 'steada Moe's brother Alfred next door."

steep

1. Expensive

> "Three ninety-five for a cup of coffee. That's some steep."
> "It's fancy coffee. They call it latte. Costs extra for the latte."

2. An angle that falls closer to vertical than horizontal

If you climb Mount Lafayette using the Greenleaf Trail, the last 200 yards or so are some steep, much like climbing stairs. The view from the top is worth the effort, should you survive. In high school, I climbed Lafayette with the Science Club. It was challenging. My friend Kevin French said: "There's slow, slower, and then there's Becky pace."

Olive Tardiff, a fine writer from Brentwood, offers this insight into the relativity of steepness: "While my husband was hiking in the White Mountains (and I was acting as backup, keeping house in our VW camper), I had occasion to go to a country store for supplies. There I found a few hangers-on near the counter, gabbing with the storekeeper. As I waited, a young man—obviously a hiker, with a big backpack—came in and said he was about to tackle a nearby mountain. He asked if it was very steep. 'Steep!' replied the storekeeper, 'Why, if anything, it leans forward a little!' "

sticklah

A sticklah won't give; a sticklah stickles to the letter of the law.

Town officials tend to be sticklahs. Say you've lived in town all your life (so far), and you get a new vehicle, but neglect to affix a new dump sticker. If your dump master is a sticklah, she'll turn you and your 15 bags of garbage away and grin while she's doing it. Even if she is your second cousin once removed.

A woman moves to New Hampshire from New York and wants to get a passport. The notary public, a sticklah, needs to see her license. Well, it's a New York license, so that won't do. A week later the woman returns with a New Hampshire license. The sticklah's pleased, but now needs to see the woman's birth certificate. A couple days later, the woman brings in her birth certificate, but it has her maiden name on it—so now the sticklah needs to see a marriage license. "Why didn't you tell me that last time I was in?" the woman said. Sticklah says, "Hadn't got that far yet."

stickled

To be the victim of a sticklah

Bob Kent got stickled at the former Pease Air Force Base. A veteran, he needed to make an appointment for his annual physical on the base. He happened to be in Newington, so he thought, why not save a phone call and stop in at the office. He found the right office (not easy), and asked the receptionist to make an appointment for him. She said she didn't make appointments except over the phone. He'd have to call. After some hemming and hawing, she pointed him down the hall to a pay phone.

He deposited his coin, dialed the number. He could hear the phone ringing in the office but no answer. He hung up, walked back down the hall. There sat the sticklah. "Why didn't you answer the phone?" he asked.

She said, "I'm on my ten-minute break."

stick to your knittin'

Tend to your own business and keep your nose out of other folks'

Easier said than done, especially in small towns where news travels fast and we have long memories. Maude says, "Maybe I should say something to Cousin Joey about that woman he's been going around with. You know, I heard she drinks like a fish."

"Or, maybe, Maude, you should stick to your knittin'."

At the annual meeting of the New England Hand Spinners Association, I heard about Buster, who had a bad back. April visited

Buster and his wife, Joyce, every summer at their place. April was a very good knitter. Since Buster was laid out with a bad back, Joyce thought April might teach him to knit. So she did.

When she returned the following summer, Buster had knit up a storm: scarves, table runners, shawls, and blankets. But he still had a bad back.

"Buster," April said, "I think you're ready to purl."

Buster agreed. Next summer, Buster greeted April with more scarves, table runners, shawls, and blankets—plus a box of socks, hats, and mittens. Joyce said: "We won't have to do any Christmas shopping at all this year."

"How's your back, Buster?" April asked.

"Better," he said, "but I've got carpal tunnel in both hands."

Buster stuck to his knittin' too much.

still-fishing

Angling from an anchored boat

Gives new meaning to the old saying, "Sometimes I sits and thinks. Sometimes I just sits." You sit and watch your bobba, hoping it'll bob under the water, signaling a bite, and then you reel in. Sometimes you sit for a very long time and the bobba never moves. Still, you never know when a fish will show interest in the nightwalker on the hook. So you sit some more. Sometimes, if you're of age, you drink be-ah to pass the time.

Still-fishing is the Yankee version of yoga—highly contemplative.

stoah-boughten

Purchased from a retailer rather than homemade

If you listen carefully at church suppers, you can hear the whispers: "I wouldn't bothah with the pecan pie. It's stoah-boughten."

stockin's

Socks

At Christmas, some hang their stockin's by the fireplace. At my childhood home, having no fireplace and only small stockin's, my brother Robit and I pinned paper bags to the overstuffed chair. Worked just as good.

stove up

Badly injured or broken

"Heard the Clement boy had an accident."
"Flew over the handlebars of his bike. He's all stove up."
You can also stave up a car.
"Elmer's brakes let go on Blake's Hill, and now his cah's all stove up."

stubbun

Set in one's ways; intractable; bull-headed; unwilling to compromise

Yankees, like any other nationality, can be stubbun. At Wilmot town meeting some years ago, I'm told, a suggestion was made to erect a new and updated veterans' monument. Seems they were a few wars behind. Discussion ensued. The monument was a fine idea, but should it be erected in Wilmot Center or Wilmot Flat? The vote tied at 85 for the Center, 85 for the Flat.

So they didn't build it.

Evidently, cool heads later prevailed. Two smaller monuments were erected on either side of the old one, bringing the rolls of Wilmot veterans up-to-date.

such a thing as knowing how
Training helps

Itinerant piano tuner Howard N. Chase of Hancock recounted many true adventures in his book, *Country Piano Tuner: His Stupid Song*. It's chock-full of sayings and stories.

He wrote: "A grandmother on the outskirts of Concord called for me to work on the family piano, and was very insistent on my coming promptly. I found out why when I got there: She had removed the keys in order to clean out the dirt under them, had put them back in the wrong order, and had one left over. My first step was to get them back where they belonged. The grandmother looked on and inquired, 'How come they go in place so easy for you, when I had such a hard time with them?' She had waded far beyond her depth and then hollered for help, so I felt impelled to rub it in a little and replied, 'There's such a thing as knowing how.' "

sugar bush
Ache-ridge populated with sugar maples

In Wolfeboro during the 1980s a fellow from away moved to town and, come sugaring time, noticed neighbors hanging buckets on trees up and down his road. So he scampered down to the hardware store, and bought a couple of taps and two shiny buckets, which he hung on the biggest tree in his front yard.

The neighbors never mentioned his sugaring effort directly, but instead would slow down as they passed his house, lean out their car windows, and laugh. Even worse, his buckets came up empty.

To this day, town folks ask how much sap he's getting out of that big old oak.

sugarhouse
A building where maple sap is boiled into syrup, or, if you boil it even longer, sugar; sometimes called a sugaring house, sap house, or sugar shack

174

Sap drips out of the tree clear and turns brown as it's boiled down, so the question from the lady from Baltimore—"When do you put the brown in?"—stumps the syrup maker.

Another visitor said, upon viewing the clear liquid in the trough, "I thought maple syrup was brown."

"That," the syrup maker said, "is your Vermont maple syrup."

In Orford, near the Vermont line, the tourist asked, "What's the difference between New Hampshire and Vermont maple syrup?"

"About ten miles."

Sundy
The first or last day of the week, depending on how you figure it; followed by Mundy, Tuesdy, Winsdy, Thursdy, Frydy, and Saddy

supposably
Expresses doubt

"Manfred supposably will have that chimbley patched by Sundy, but I'm not holding my breath."

suthin' the rats overlooked
A snack

"Welcome t' set down with me and have a bite. Haven't got any bread; she forgot t' get any last night, but we've got some beans, and I guess I can find some crackers, or suthin' the rats overlooked." This was the exact wording of an invitation extended to Howard Chase, itinerant piano tuner, in his travels.

swamp donkey
A moose

Grace Enman of Milan met her first moose in downtown Berlin. She was just a little girl. She accompanied her father to a lawyer's office in one of the big buildings on Main Street. Grace held her father's hand as they walked up three flights of stairs. He sat her in a big chair in the waiting room while he attended to business. Grace was so small that her legs dangled. Then she looked, and across the room saw the great antlers and head and eyes and nose of a moose on the wall. She thought the rest of it was in the next office.

swamp Yankee
Lives in the lowlands and stores appliances and car parts in the door yard, since they might come in handy down the road

swipe
Steal

"At the swimming hole, I left my wallet under a towel on the front seat of the Buick and somebody swiped it."

"Musta been some dink from outatown."

switchel
A cooling beverage favored by the Shakers, according to Mary Boswell in her book, Seasoned with Grace

To prepare, stir together and chill: 4 cups brown sugar, 2 cups molasses, 2 teaspoons ginger, 2 gallons water, and 2 cups vinegar. Non-Shakers sometimes add rum.

swole
Variation of swell

Bug bites swole up. So do twisted ankles and the heads of people who think quite a lot of themselves. "After Winston got named 'Septage Hauler of the Year,' his head got so swole he couldn't fit through the door."

"The brook's so swole from the spring runoff, it's going ova the bridge steada under it."

T

ta

"At" spelled backwards; means at; or to

Lena LaPierre split her own kindling into her late 80s. She lived next door to her daughter, Lillian, and family. One day, Lena appeared at the door. "Anybody ta home?" she called. Luckily somebody was. She'd cut her thumb with the hatchet. The thumb was dangling by a thread and she was holding the pieces together with a bloody towel.

After that, they hid the hatchet.

taht

1. Not sweet

Ma presented an apple pie with a perfect hole in the center.

"I forgot the sugar," she said. "I put some in after with a funnel, but it might be a little taht."

Pa lifted the crust, sprinkled sugar over the whole pie, and called it good.

2. Wild woman

In some parts of the world, like England, a woman with loose morals is called a taht. We're a tolerant people so we don't call them such names as that. But, on rare occasions when I slather on lipstick and powder my face, I call it "getting tahted up," which I suppose relates to the English usage.

t'ain't

Opposite of 'tis

At the lumber camp, the cook carved T. M. into the crust of his pies. When asked what the letters stood for, he said, " 'Tis meat or t'ain't meat—you decide."

takin' a tub

Bathing

The plumber arrived at the house ready to tackle the clogged sink.

"Bathroom's the second door on the right," the owner said. "Go in quick and pull the door tight behind you. Muhtha's takin a tub, and if there's a draft she'll be some cross."

tastes like more

Delicious

"How's the bluebry cobbler?"

"Tastes like more."

taxes

We pay 'em, but we don't enjoy it.

Experts say New Hampshire has one of the lowest tax burdens in the country. Maybe so, but when that property tax bill comes in, you'd be hard-pressed to get anybody to believe it.

In Loudon, the newcomer who'd moved up from Dunstable, Massachusetts, unloaded on the town clerk one afternoon. He raved about how much he loved Dunstable and how lacking Loudon was: no streetlights, no kindergarten, the roads don't get plowed, no trash pickup.

"If you dislike Loudon so much," the town clerk said, "why'd you move here?"

"Low taxes."

In another town, the new landowner complained about his taxes. "Why, that lot's not worth anywhere near what you say it is," he said to the selectman. "Half of it's swamp and the other half's ledge. There's a power line through the middle, not to mention a right-of-way to the neighboring lot."

The selectman was unmoved: "If it's such a lousy piece of property, what'd you buy it for?"

A big-shot bank president attended his first and last town meeting. He ranted about the high taxes, and how even he couldn't afford to live here.

Fella says, "Hope you brought your suitcase."

teeta-totta

Seesaw

When a child on one end of the plank, balanced on a fulcrum, pushes up, the other end goes down. Up and down, up and down. If the trusting child is up high and the mean child jumps off, the trusting child's tailbone gets bruised.

tell us some lies, Huey

A request for stories

I don't know who Huey is, or, more likely, was, but he must have been an accomplished spinner of yarns. At the contra dance, when folks are tuckered out from stepping, swinging, and do-si-do-ing, somebody says, "Tell us some lies, Huey," and the storyteller in the group holds forth.

Of course, Huey always prefaces his or her tale with the line, "This is a true story."

theme pahk

A place for entertainment

Phil Chapman of Newport nostalgically recalled the days of the open-burn dump: "You could take your girlfriend out there to this secluded place at night, then go back the next day and shoot rats. Kinda like a rural teenager's theme pahk."

things you see when you don't have a gun

Horrors; this is sometimes used ironically to mean not horrible at all, but attractive. Variation: Things you see when you don't have a gun or a camera.

The newcomer to town, unaware of local customs, lies in the sun on her front lawn wearing nothing but a bikini and a big hat. An old fella walks by. His comment: "The things you see when you don't have a gun." She took it as a compliment.

It's true though. You are apt to see the moose beside the road when you don't have a gun. The flock of wild turkeys crosses the road in front of your pickup when you don't have a gun. The 12-point buck eats apples under your in-laws' tree, as you watch through the window, having just finished Sunday dinner, when you don't have a gun.

thon

Needlelike protrusion from a stem

Roses and blackberries have thons. An attractive woman standing between two homely men is said to be "a rose between thons."

thongs

Before a pair of skimpy underwear was called a thong, we wore thongs to the beach on our feet (also called flip-flops).

three-kegger

Poor construction

Look closely at the floor of the Unity town hall and you'll see some boards are laid straight, but a good many are laid crooked. This is a three-kegger floor. The more cider the volunteers drank, the crookeder the floorboards went down.

tickled
Pleased

"Ida was some tickled when she found the keys between the couch cushions. She thought somebody'd swiped 'em."

tighter than a clam in a cat's paw
Very tight

When clams sense danger, they close their shells. How the cat got ahold of that clam, now that's a puzzlement.

tighter than the bark on a tree
Sensibly frugal

"When Old Ned died, he had more than a million dollars socked away in the bank."

"No wonder. He was tighter than the bark on a tree."

times
By the time

"Times we got to the church, the wedding was all over."

tippin' a few
Drinking alcoholic beverages

Mary Jane Ogmundson of Wilmot takes a walk early each morning. She says, "When I find beer cans or bottles I pick them up to bring home to dispose of properly. One morning I neglected to bring a plastic bag, so I was holding a can in each hand as I headed home. A native fella pulled up in his truck, rolled down the window, and yelled, 'You're tippin' a few a bit early, ain't ya?' "

tithing man

Collector of donated money

George Wells in South Sutton maintains the tradition of collecting contributions from the congregation on Old Home Day at the meetinghouse.

George'll tickle you with his feather on a stick if you don't fork over when the plate is passed. And if you should try to slip in a wooden nickel, he'll hold it high for all to see. Sometimes he bites silver dollars, to make sure they're real. He's a pistol, and so's his son, Jody, the assistant tithing man.

toasta

Appliance in which you brown up your bread

In Colebrook, a cabin rental place went out of business and the contents were sold off at auction, including dozens of toastas going for 25 cents each. Spencer bought one.

"Spencer," said the woman sitting next to him, "you didn't get a cod with your toasta."

Spencer said, "Don't need one. Don't have electricity."

tolerant

Willing to live and let live

Yankees are a tolerant people. We have to be. We have a lot to put up with.

Sydney, an Alstead farmer and a local character, was visited by a couple and their little boy. He said to the husband: "You have brown hair. Your wife has brown hair. But your boy has red hair. How'd that happen?"

The father said, "My neighbor has red hair."

Sydney said: "If it's all right with you, then it's all right with me."

tonic

Soda pop, cola; a sweet carbonated drink

"Reach in the cooler, wouldja, Freda, and get me a be-ah, and a tonic for yourself."

toock

From the French toque, a knit hat

"Olivier put on his parka, wrapped his scarf around his neck, pulled his toock over his ears, mittened up, and set off down the trail."

too small, too fah away

1. *An excuse for not shooting a deah offered up by hunters trying to explain why, once again, despite spotting a deah or two, they've returned empty-handed*

Toad says: "I saw three does in Paltry's meadow."
"Why dint you shoot 'em?"
"Too small, too fah away."

2. *Can also be used more generally to explain non-hunting near-misses*

"Did you get the job with the phone company?"
"Nope. Too small, too fah away."

t'othah

Other; used for comparison

"Is your kitten a boy cat or a girl cat?"
"One or t'othah."

tougher than a boiled owl

Difficult to chew; boiled owl is even tougher than boiled eel

"Did you enjoy the steak?"
"Mostly gristle and tougher than a boiled owl. But tasty."

town clerk

An elected official who issues dump stickers, dog licenses, car registrations, and beach passes; more importantly, THE most powerful person in town

The professor had just moved to Derry. He went into the town hall and spoke to a woman behind the desk at the selectmen's office.

"How do I get permission to raise swine?" he asked.

"For that, you'll have to check with the town clerk."

"Who is the town clerk?"

"Me."

town meeting

When the residents of a town come together, usually on a Tuesday evening or Saturday morning in March, to vote on how to fund the various municipal departments and projects

Discussion is encouraged. A moderator, elected by the town, tries to keep discourse civil. It's hard. Moderators often say: "I will not tolerate personal attacks," to which townsfolk reply, "Damn. Those are the best kind."

Town meeting can run an hour or 12, depending on the number of articles, the number of ballot votes called for, the swiftness of the moderator's tongue, and the mood of the voters. If it's Saturday morning and the high school has a championship basketball game scheduled for that afternoon, town meeting moves right along. If it starts to snow, the votes go faster than the falling flakes.

Otherwise, town meeting has a tendency to drag.

A number of towns have done away with town meeting by instituting what is known as Senate Bill 2 (SB2). Instead of meeting on the third Saturday in March to vote the town budget and warrant articles, a so-called Deliberative Session is held some random time in February or March so people can talk about the budget and articles, amend them if they so desire, but no vote up or down is taken. That has to wait for voting day at a later date.

Generally, nobody much shows up at Deliberative Sessions, aka, Town Meeting Without Teeth.

traffic circle
A four-corners that's been turned into a roundabout

In New Hampshire, and this is important, the cars already in the circle have the right of way. That is, the cars just entering the circle ought to back off and let the ones go who are already in. Evidently in other states, like Massachusetts, the opposite applies. This causes problems.

traipse
To walk around, usually in the woods, without a particular purpose

"What's Ethel up to?"
"Traipsing around the back fawty."

travis
A large, handmade sled

"That travis, loaded down with twelve riders, got going so fast on Colby Hill that when the one in front screamed, the one in back never heard it."

tree squeak
A small, seldom-seen member of the weasel family

As you walk through the woods, if you hear a squeak overhead and look up, but see nothing except bare branches, it's probably a tree squeak. Tree squeaks are most active on windy days.

tripe
The lining of a cow's stomach, fried or boiled, and served in diners; a Northern New England delicacy

trust-fund babies

Newcomers with no obvious source of income

If people don't go to work every day or have a sign advertising a business out front of their house, we wonder how they support themselves. Must come from money, we figure. Either that, or they're Mafia.

Generally, locals look askance at trust-fund babies.

truth be told

Actually

"I caught a twelve-inch bass right off the dock. Well, truth be told, I hooked him, but he fell off before I could net him."

In some cases, "truth be told" signals a lie.

tuckered out

Exhausted

If I climbed Mount Washington, I'd get all tuckered out, so I'd rather ride the Cog.

tuner

Albacore

"The fella who's fixing the piano is staying for lunch, so I'm making tuner sandwiches."

tunk

Heavier than a tap, lighter than a hit; also, good tunk, which amounts to about a tunk and a half

"Valve's stuck again."
"Give it a tunk."
"Still stuck."
"Give it a good tunk."
"That did the trick, Ollie."

turned

Soured; gone bad

Milk turns. Week-old kung pao chicken has likely turned and should be put in the basket. Susan ate a hot dog that had been left in the trunk of the car all night. It was a warm night. She got sick.

When sick people get sicker, they take turns for the worse.

t'weren't

Past tense of t'wan't; were not

Fred Creed's father, who enjoyed a fine meal, said of a restaurant at which he'd recently dined: "T'weren't so bad but what I haven't et worse."

twist

Soft-serve frozen confection on a cone; it's not ice cream, but similar. This is called a creamee in Vermont, and a dairy joy in Down East Maine.

In Quebec, they call them tweests.

two-seater

An outhouse with room for two; also, three-seater, four-seater, ten-seater, and so forth.

Medora Snigger said that in the logging camps a person might have to step over the knees of several persons before finding an open seat in the multi-seater outhouse.

"Wasn't that embarrassing?"

"We didn't mind," she said. "It was the only chance we had to sit and visit."

U and V

uglier than a bag of smashed apples

Unattractive

Upon seeing Maggie's dachsund/bulldog cross, Lester said, "By gawd, that little dog's run his legs clean off."

But he didn't say, "And, he's uglier than a bag of smashed apples." That would have been insensitive.

ugly

In a foul mood

Sheree woke up ugly because somebody spilled grape juice on the kitchen floor in the night, didn't clean it up, and it was a big sticky mess.

Often used in the expression, "don't that make me ugly":

"Those solicitors calling up at suppertime trying to sell me a warrantee for a cah I don't own—don't that make me ugly."

"Some ugly" is even uglier than ugly: "When Cecil found out the boy run his snow machine into the stone wall and stove it all to hell, he was some ugly."

'um

Them; sometimes written as 'em, but said aloud as 'um

"Give 'um hell, Nell."

unthaw

Thaw; you'd think "unthaw" would mean freeze, but it don't.

up Maine

The big state to our north and east

"When Toodie wants a bahgin on chocolate bahs, she goes up Maine to Renys. When her sista from Augusta wants a bahgin on alcohol, she visits Toodie in New Hampshire."

Means about the same as down Maine. Ain't that a puzzlement?

use everything but the squeal

To be frugal

A frugal farmer who raises a pig uses every part of that pig except the squeal.

use it up, wear it out, make it do, or do without

Yankee philosophy

Several people suggested this adage as an old New Hampshire saying, but it's probably been said in lots of places, and dates back to the Depression at least.

varies

Changes; short, noncommittal answer to an unanswerable question

The tourists climbed Mount Monadnock (the second-most-climbed mountain in the world, right behind Mount Fuji) and encountered the fire warden who manned the lookout up top.

"How many fires do you spot from here in a year?" the tourists asked.

"Varies."

view tax

A particularly annoying tax, since "view" is in the eye of the beholder; if a property sits up high and has a pleasing vista, the taxes go up.

Jim had a house in Boscawen, up high overlooking a dairy farm and, beyond the farm, the Merrimack River. In the spring of the year, when the farmer dressed his fields, the odor was pungent.

Jim got assessed a view tax. He agreed he had a view all right. "From where I sit, I got a view and a pee-yew."

In New London, which has some lovely hills and valleys, the fellow complained that his lot and house were just about the same as his neighbor's down the road. "Same size house," he complained to a selectman. "Same acreage. Same driveway. Same big rock sitting in the middle of the lawn. How come my taxes are higher?"

The selectman said, "Because your rock has a view."

In Deerfield, the joke going around (at least I think it was a joke) is that the folks on the hill behind the lake, whose woods got flattened in the spring tornado of 2008, were stunned to see their taxes go up.

Upon inquiry, they were told: "Ahcowuss your taxes went up—now you have a view."

village

A congregation of buildings considered the town center

Often, but not always, the village includes a church or two, a general store, library, historical society, a cemetery, town hall, and post office. Sometimes there's a town green and a gazebo. When someone says, "I'm going to the village," they're headed out to do errands, go to a meeting, or volunteer at the historical society.

visit

1. To go to someone's house and spend time with them

2. To converse, as in, "Carol's quite a talker; she loves to visit."

W

waggin

Almost anything with four wheels

A car: "Load up the waggin and we'll head to the beach."

A baby carriage: "Put the baby in the waggin. Mumma's gonna walk down street."

A grocery cart: "I went in for milk and eggs and came out with a waggin full."

wahm

Neither hot, nor cold, nor cool; a relative term

In January, if the temperature breaks 40, the day's considered wahm—time to open the windows and air out the house. In August, anything below 60 seems cool. Time to bundle up and start a blaze in the fireplace.

This wahmed my heart. After a storytelling session in Wilmot in January, as I was signing books, a stranger asked for my car keys. I didn't think twice and handed 'em over. She said, "Tell me what your cah looks like and I'll go out and staht it up so it'll be wahm." Good thing. The thermometer on the rearview mirror read 8-below when I pulled out of town hall yard.

wa'n't

Was not or wasn't

The woman who lived in the house at the end of the road always intended to stop in and introduce herself to the folks who bought the house at the beginning of the road, just two miles away. But she got busy; time passed.

One day driving by, she noticed a sign for maple syrup out front and decided this was a good chance to stop in. She bought a gallon and introduced herself. "How long have you folks been living here?" she said.

"Seven years."

"I'm mawtified," the woman said. "I should have stopped in long before this to welcome you to the neighborhood."

"Don't worry," the neighbor said. "We wa'n't waiting for you."

whackin' pile

A lot

"We sold a whackin' pile of junk at the flea mahket."

whatever blows your skirt up

Whatever excites you; indicates tolerance

"I really enjoy Formula One racing."

"Oh, yuh? Whatever blows your skirt up."

what the hell you doing here?

Affectionate Yankee greeting when an unexpected visitor arrives

what took ya

A question meaning, Were you, perhaps, delayed? Or, Mightn't you have hurried a little, under the circumstances?

Bruce Geiger's neighbor in Lyneborough told me this story. Bruce recently died, but is fondly remembered as a great Yankee character. A tall thin man, good with horses, did a lot of work in the woods.

One day he was out in the woods working with his tricycle tractor. When his wife came home from the village, Bruce hadn't returned. She got ahold of their other neighbor, Tinker Anderson. "Tinkah," she said, "I haven't seen Bruce. He should have been home hours ago."

So Tinker went in search of Bruce and came upon a terrible scene: the tractor upended and Bruce pinned underneath. He rushed to Bruce's side, expecting the worse.

Bruce looked up, blinked, and said: "What took ya?"

when it does

A good answer to a poor question, as in: "When do you think the ice will go out on Sunapee?"

"When it does."

Similiar to "always has befoah."

"Do you think it'll ever stop raining?"

"Always has befoah."

where the hell you been?

Affectionate Yankee greeting when a visitor arrives more than one minute later than expected

"Where the hell you been?"

"Had to stop for a flock of wild turkeys in the road at the bottom of the hill."

"They'll disappear soon as the law comes off."

whyn't

Why don't? Or wouldn't it be a good idea if?

"Chippa shredda broke."

"Whyn't you take it up to Stubby? He fixed mine up slick when it slipped a cog last fall."

"Good idear."

wicked

1. Extra

More prevalent in Maine than New Hampshire, but you hear it some in the Granite State. And in Massachusetts, too. Sometimes

193

we use it when we're trying to pass as Mainuhs, like when we're in Maine. Sign on the road in the North Country: WICKED GOOD LATTES AHEAD. I'm pretty sure that was composed by a flatlander.

Something can be wicked good, like those lattes, or wicked bad, like a thunderstorm that shakes the house.

2. Evil

I suppose somebody could be wicked wicked if they were especially wicked. But that just seems like overkill.

A wicked nice lady in Loudon told how a minister in town tried his darnedest to get her father to attend church. Father said: "When I get to feeling wicked, I'll be down."

widow-maker

A heavy, dead limb apt to fall off and turn a logger's spouse into a widow

Helen Burns, lady logger, described a close encounter: "I had this stick come down one time. I wore them dungarees that had that ruler pocket on the side. Limb come down and tore that pocket right off."

willies

Shivery feeling something bad might happen

"The owl screeching outside my window gave me the willies."

Probably not related to the story of the Willey House, but maybe. In 1826, the rumblings of a landslide frightened the Willey family from their home in Crawford Notch. They ran, it's surmised, for the root cellar, some distance away. All were killed in the slide, but the house was untouched. A boulder behind the house split the slide in two and protected it. If they'd stayed put they would have been fine.

Just thinking about it gives me the willies.

willing team

A team of hosses or oxen or people that works well together

Ernest Mack tells of sisters Bernice and Persis, who made a willing team. "Bernice was willing to do all the work and Persis was willing to let her."

willy-nilly

Catch as catch can, helter-skelter, chaotic

At town meeting, a resident complained about the state of her road. It needed work. All humps and bumps, washouts, and frost heaves. Roads across town were getting fixed, but not hers. "Is there a plan for improving the roads in town," she demanded, "or is it willy-nilly?"

The road agent went to the mic and replied, with dignity: "It's willy-nilly."

Wilmot standards

High indeed; if something's just as it should be, it meets Wilmot standards; most things do not.

In Wilmot, a neighbor came down with the epizudic, so Karen took him a casserole to tide him over. The next week she returned for the dish.

"How'd you like it?" she asked, forgetting the rule that you never ask a Yankee a question unless you're prepared for an honest answer.

The neighbor said: "T'wan't up to Wilmot standards."

winnah

Used in the ironic sense, "He's a winnah," means he's not apt to win a prize.

At the party, J. P. made an awful face. "What's the matter," his friend asked. "You having a heart attack or what?"

J. P. pointed to the bowl on the little table. He'd grabbed a handful of potpourri and munched it. After considerable spitting and choking, he managed to say: "I thought they were be-ah nuts."

J. P., in that moment, was a winnah.

woodchuck

Groundhog; despised because they eat gardens; they don't just nibble, they eat everything.

Also called whistle pigs. Andy Robert explains: "The key to hunting whistle pigs, as taught to me by my dad, formerly a rabid woodchuck assassin, is if you shoot and miss, go immediately to their hole and whistle loudly. About seven times out of ten the whistle pig will stick his or her head out of the hole and whistle back, at which point you pull the trigger.

"Compassionate whistle pig killers will use the trick only after June, because in April and May you're likely to kill a mother still nursing her brood. Killing chucks with a bullet is one thing; starving 'em is another."

woods queer

A little mad from staying too long in the woods

Norma Oleson said: "My husband was a logging superintendent for Brown Company, responsible for building the roads, hiring the men. He opened Bog Brook and lived at Parmachenee. Stan Wensel came by one day and found me and my son Ola, a little baby, sitting in the car, making noises, pretending to drive. He said to my husband: 'I think she's getting woods queer. You better take her out.' "

wood wahms you twice

It wahms you when you're harvesting it as well as when you burn it.

The stove salesman told Roy: "This stove will use half the wood of any other stove and keep you just as wahm."

Roy said, "I'll take two."

"Two?"

"Sure. Then I won't have to cut any wood at all."

work like a bugger

To do a job fast and with intensity

"How'd you get that roof shingled in just one day, Scrappy?"

"I worked like a bugger."

work up

To turn a tree into firewood: fell, limb, cut to length, and split

The invention of the chain saw made working up wood a lot easier. Before chain saws, trees were felled by hand with crosscut saws. Lloyd was the first in Dummer to try a chain saw. After a week, he returned it to the fella who'd sold it to him.

"This chain saw's no good. I do better with the crosscut. I can usually work up three cods in a day. With this, just half a cod."

"Is it working properly?" the fella said. He pulled the starter cord and the chain saw roared to life.

Lloyd jumped back: "What's that noise?"

A related term, buck up, may date to the use of buck saws.

worst weather in the world

The weather at the top of Mount Washington

When the temperature drops, the snow comes, and the wind picks up, it can get downright inhospitable at the peak. Storms come up fast and brutal. Temperatures plummet and the wind blows hard. The second-highest ground wind ever recorded blew across the top of Mount Washington in 1934. That wind was blowing 231 miles per hour and the record held for decades.

Where was the highest wind speed recorded and when? We don't give a hoot.

wove

Waved

"I went to stop at the light but the cop wove me on through."

wunchano

"Wouldn't you know" said fast

I heard it in Troy and thought, yup, that's how we say it. Here's the story that elicited a couple of wunchanos.

Clyde Huntoon (pronounced Hontoon) of Fitzwilliam was quite a character. Seems the locals formed a reenactment militia in 1976 to celebrate the U.S. bicentennial, and were invited to Fort Ticonderoga for a battle. The Troy/Fitzwilliam contingent owned a cannon in working condition. They'd fill it with powder and touch 'er off on special occasions.

At Ticonderoga in the heat of the mock battle, wunchano, Clyde—in charge of the cannon—got a little bored. So as the redcoats, in their beautiful (and expensive) red coats charged up the hill, Clyde loaded a cow flop (evidently, the battle took place in a pasture) into the cannon and let it fly.

The redcoats were thoroughly sprayed.

Ticked off and spotted with cow flop flak, the redcoats captured the cannon—and, wunchano, didn't give it back for five years.

At the historical society meeting, Gladys was fondly remembered. Angus, society president, was happy to report the dear lady got her wish.

"What wish was that?" Lizzie asked.

"After she died, she wanted to be shot out of our cannon," Angus said. "Wunchano, it took three shots."

"Oh, my," Lizzie said. "Was she cremated?"

wunt
Will not

Walter Sanborn took his two boys for a swim in the river. Time to leave and the boys wouldn't get out of the water. Walter said, "If you two don't behave, next time I bring you, you wunt come."

Wyowa
Midwestern state; its state capital is Away.

A good number of people from away call Wyowa home.

Y

yahd sale

Garage sale, tag sale, barn sale

A door-yard event where you sell stuff you don't want to people looking for bargains.

People who attend yahd sales are said to be yahd sailing.

Yankee

I heard this from Jud Hale, longtime Yankee *magazine editor and raconteur, but the definition of "Yankee" has probably been passed along among storytellers and refined over time. To folks on other continents, a Yankee is an American. In the southern United States, a Yankee is someone who lives north of the Mason-Dixon Line. North of the Mason-Dixon Line, a Yankee is someone, usually with deep roots and English or Scottish heritage, from Maine, New Hampshire, or Vermont. In Maine, New Hampshire, and Vermont, a Yankee is someone who eats pie for breakfast.*

Yankee is also an attitude, easily determined with a few simple tests.

Test One:

How would you answer the question, "Do you know how to get to Barnstead?"

If your answer is, "Ayuh," you've got the Yankee attitude.

Test Two:

"How long does it take to get to Hudson?"

Yankee answer: "Depends on how fast you go."

Test Three:

Angler on the lake says, "Sir, would you show me where the rocks are?"

Yankee answer: "No, but I'll show you where they ain't."

Test Four:

"Can I help with that?"

Yankee answer: "No, it's hahd enough alone."

Yankee hug

Consists of standing side by side about a foot apart, arms crossed, then turning your heads so you're looking into one another's eyes. Nod.

In Hill, Martha Jordan approached me at the start of a story-telling session and said she needed to give me a hug. Being of Yankee extraction, I stiffened right up. Being of Yankee extraction herself, Martha was a little stiff, too, but we got the job done.

I asked why she needed to give me a hug. She said: "I know you better now!"

Evidently, last time I was in Hill—a couple years ago—I asked Martha if she'd help me demonstrate a Yankee hug. She declined, saying: "I don't know you well enough."

The Yankee and his grandson, the littlest Yankee, were riding through town in the pickup. The Yankee saw a person on the side of the road he knew, so he waved. The person didn't wave back.

"That wasn't very nice," the Yankee said. "He didn't even wave back."

The littlest Yankee said, "He nodded."

Yankee humor

Understatement understated; stories delivered with as few words and as little description as possible, just the bare bones leading up to a true-to-life punch line that's so subtle you might not even realize it was a punch line

Practitioners of Yankee humor are often described as dry. The masters deliver their lines straightfaced and monotoned. Often it's the delivery that creates the humor—the way the words snap off the tongue.

With some of the best Yankee humor, people don't laugh until an hour later. Or a week. Here's one from Daniel Webster Harvey of Epping: "When the old maid got married, folks said, 'That was sudden.' "

Storyteller and fiddler Harvey Tolman of Nelson delivered this story without even the hint of a smile: While having coffee with a friend, Harvey noticed three holes cut in the dustboards of the kitchen right through to the outside. "What are those holes for?" he asked.

"For the cats."

"How many cats do you have?"

"Three."

"Why can't the cats all use one hole?"

"Because when I say scat, I mean scat."

Yankee trader

A wily businessperson who always comes out on top in a deal

The classic example is the hoss trader who cajoles a buyer saying, "Old Nellie doesn't look too good, but she's strong and she's got a lot of work left in her."

202

The man pays $50 for Old Nellie, but brings her back the next day: "You tricked me! Old Nellie walked right off the road into the ditch. That hoss is blind."

To which the trader replies, "I told you she didn't look too good."

Linwood Rogers, farmer and Yankee trader, sold picnic tables in Canterbury for $16 each. Fella says, "Linwood, how long does it take you to make one of those picnic tables?"

" 'Bout four hours."

"Four hours," the fella kellates. "Sixteen dollahs. That's about four dollahs an hour, ain't it?"

Linwood agreed that it was.

The fella says, "Can you make me a picnic table for three dollahs an hour?"

"Shoe-uh," Linwood says, "but it'll take a little longer."

yass
Rhymes with sass; affirmative, but with a degree of dismay

"Your mother-in-law gonna visit again this summer?"

"Yass. Her and the wife got all kinds of stuff planned, and damned if it don't interfere with fishin'."

"Whyn't you go to camp and hide out?"

"The thought has crossed my mind."

ye-ah
Twelve months makes one

yogut

Made from milk and sometimes flavored with fruit

If you eat too much yogut, yo gut might expand.

New Hampshire's own Stonyfield Farm company started with a cow and a pail and is now bullish in the field.

your personality is showing

A polite way of saying a man has forgotten to zip his fly after shaking the dew off his lily

Gazetteer

Place Names and Pronunciations, So You'll Know Where You Are and How to Say It

New Hampshire boasts many colorful place names, suggestive of history, geography, attitude, and humor. In this uncomprehensive list, I've included the controversial ones. How do you pronounce Boscawen or Umbagog? Darned if I know, and I grew up in Boscawen. In my travels, I've inquired many times about *UM-bah-gog* versus *Um-BAY-gog.* The debate rages on.

Ginger Jannenga of East Colebrook reminds us: "Up here when you ask where someone lives, you often get the name of an area or neighborhood versus the town and street. Like up in Pittsburg, people live in places like Back Lake, First Lake, or Indian Stream. In Stewartstown, they may live in Bear Rock or Creampoke, or Diamond Pond. In Columbia, they live out in Bungy or on Marshall Hill. You've lived in Colebrook quite a while and become one of the natives if you give directions that include places like Kidderville, Upper Kidderville, Four Corners, Cooper Hill, and Factory Village."

Following Ginger's lead, I've included areas as well as towns, mountains, bodies of waters, and roads. Old names you might not find on any map. Names that make me smile, like Effingham. Some names are included not because they're tricky to pronounce, but because they've got stories attached that seem worth telling.

We'll start with A for Alstead.

Alstead

Pronounced just like it's spelled: Al-stead. *Locals say, "There's no all in Alstead."*

A couple from away bought a piece of land by the river in Alstead to build a retirement home when the time came. After the flood, they drove up to see how their plot had fared. They stood on a bridge overlooking the river and saw that their land was inundated. A local couple stood beside them, also surveying the damage.

"Who are you?" the local couple asked.

"We own three acres down there."

"Oh, so you're the damn fools that bought it."

Aziscohos Lake

A-ziss-co-hoss; partly in New Hampshire and partly in Maine

Ola Oleson did some traveling near Aziscohos when he was just a little tyke. His father, Alton, worked for the logging company. Ola said: "Sometimes my father would pack me on his back and take me on the job. On an average day, he might walk fifteen or twenty miles. Up in Lincoln Pond country, deep in the woods, he was spotting—marking trees. He set me down for less than two minutes. I saw a chipmunk. Ended up at Aziscohos Lake. He found me eventually, but he aged twenty years in the process. Where do you start looking when you're seventeen miles from the nearest road? 'Course, there's nothing in those woods that would hurt you."

Berlin

As in, "Burr, it's cold in Berlin come February." BURR-lin, New Hampshire, is pronounced the opposite of Ber-LIN, Germany. Also known as "The City that Trees Built" because of its long tradition of logging and mills.

Areas in Berlin include the West Side, the East Side, Cascade, and Norwegian Village.

Mount Forest, mostly bare rock towering over the West Side, looks like an elephant. Folks say, "My house is by the tail of the elephant," or by the trunk, or under the elephant's belly.

When the mills were going full swing, sometimes Berlin smelled bad because of the chemical smoke from the stacks downtown. One good thing, a native told me, "We never had any problems with mosquitoes or blackflies."

The view of the White Mountains from the top of Cate's Hill is unsurpassed.

Bethlehem
Pronounced just like the biblical place; picturesque town in the North Country with the oldest continually running movie theater in the country

Evidently, in 1799 the town fathers were trying to come up with a name for the town. It was Christmastime, so Bethlehem seemed appropriate.

Bethlehem is also home to a large Jewish population (well, large compared to the rest of the state). A woman driving slowly down a side street spotted an elderly man walking along in her same direction. He was all in black with braids and a black hat. Her son had never seen a Hassid before, so the boy kind of stared out the open window. At the stop sign, the old man caught up to the car. He said to the little boy, "What? You never saw a Yankee before?"

Bloody Point
The original name for Newington; may refer to battles between early settlers and Indians, or, in another story, boundary disputes among the settlers themselves

Boscawen

I grew up in Boscawen so I think I know how to pronounce it, but even in town, there's still debate. Here are a few pronunciations: Bos-coin, Bos-quin, Bos-quine, Bos-ca-wen, Bos-ca-wine. *But never,* Bos-COW-in.

Boscawen's named after an English lord and was the birthplace (October 16, 1806) of the famous Whig, William Pitt Fessenden. I know this because there's a rock with a plaque that says so in front of my Uncle Herb's house on King Street.

Bristol

A stranger asked the old fella on the porch at the Danbury village store, "How do you get to Bristol?"

The old fella replied, "My son-in-law usually takes me."

Broken Bridge Road

In Chichester; sounds tricky to navigate

The fella from away says, "Does this road go to Loudon?"
Nate says: "Nope. Just stays right where it is."
The fella rephrases: "Does this road end up in Loudon?"
"Ayuh."
Fella from away goes off.
Nate's buddy says: "Nate, you didn't tell that fella from away the bridge was broken."
Nate says: "He didn't ask."

Canterbury

New Hampshire is home to two historic Shaker villages, one in Canterbury, the other in Enfield. Both are well worth visiting.

Much has been written about the Shakers and their enterprising and inventive ways. 'Tis a gift to be simple, and so forth. The Shakers had four hard-and-fast rules:

1. Separation from the world
2. Confession of sin
3. United inheritance
4. A virginal or pure life

They'd probably still be thriving except for that pesky rule number four. Sexual abstinence meant no Shaker babies and, eventually, no more Shakers. The buildings remain, though, and the songs.

Carlo Mountain

In the Mahoosuc Range, it was named for a dog, Carlo, beloved companion to mountaineer E. B. Cook.

Chatham

Chat-HAM, *or, some say,* Chat-um*; it's debatable*

David Emerson calls it Chatham-New-Hampshire-sister-city-to-Stow-Maine, all one word. He should know; he grew up in Stow. Chatham's the only town in New Hampshire that you can't get to from New Hampshire. You have to go to Maine and backtrack. Well, you could take the Hurricane Mountain Road out of Conway, but most seasons it's not recommended.

Chocorua

Bald, pointy peak in the town of the same name, pronounced Chic-OR-rue-ah, *not* Chick-o-RUE-a, *which sounds to me like chewing gum.*

Named for Chief Chocorua who died on the mountain by falling, leaping, or maybe being shot by settlers. Several legends persist, but they all end the same way: a curse on the settlers and their kin.

Cockermouth River

Feeds Newfound Lake; don't get all confused and call it the Corkamouth River, because that would be wrong, and it's not even how it's spelled.

Tourists and locals alike enjoy the Sculptured Rocks in the Cockermouth, a great swimming and wading hole.

Colebrook

Way up north

In the 1930s, Judge took his car to Nugent's Garage in town for a tune-up. "How wide should I set the points?" the young fella asked. "Wide enough to drop a dime through," Judge said.

211

When he got his car back, it ran terrible. "What did you do to it?"

"Just tuned it up," the young fella said. "I didn't have a dime, though, so I used two nickels."

Concord

Our capital city, pronounced conquered. *Some say* Conkid; *that's okay, too. Just don't say* con-cord, *like the grape.*

The famous Abbot-Downing stagecoaches, the vehicle of choice in the first half of the 19th century, were also known as Concord Coaches, because they were manufactured here.

Contoocook

A town and a river

"You can't cook!"

"Con too cook."

Also called Tooky.

Coos

The quickest way to root out someone from away is to ask them to pronounce the name of our northernmost county. A dove coos. The county is Co-OS.

Coos derives from *co-ash*, an Indian word for pine.

Cornish Flat

Pronounced Connish Flat

An old-timer couldn't drive, so he asked the neighbor in Cornish Flats to take him to Claremont so he could buy day-old doughnuts. "What do you want with day-old doughnuts?" the neighbor asked.

"To keep the rats from eating the potatoes I got down cellah."

Disappearing Pond

Art Slade says this pond over near Alton "had a habit of disappearing every now and then. Finally disappeared for good about seventy-five years ago."

Dorchester

Pronounced DAW-chest-ah

Small town, population 341 last count, in our midwest—that is, out Canaan way. If you can find it, you'll enjoy it. Bring a lunch, though. There are no restaurants in Dorchester.

Dover

Pronounced Doe-vah

It's one of our earliest settlements—since 1623. Once a mill town just up the river from Portsmouth, like all mill towns, it had an odor to it, so the old saying went, "Portsmouth by the see, Dover by the smell."

Dublin

Home to Yankee *magazine and* The Old Farmer's Almanac

Everybody in Dublin speaks with an Irish accent. (Just kidding.)

Dummer

Pronounced Dummah

In neighboring Milan locals say: "Milan may be dumb, but the next town's Dummer."

This beautiful North Country town has grown steadily over the years, from 7 in 1810, the year the first census was taken, to a whopping 328 in 2007.

East Andover

Pronounced East Andova

Home to Highland Lake and the Highland Lake Inn.

Folks in surrounding towns acknowledge East Andover's rural nature by calling it East Overshoe. A lot of my relatives live in East Andover, so I thought it would be wise to include it and avoid ticking them off.

Effingham

Every time I see the sign for Effingham, pronounced Eff-in-ham, *I smile. It's my favorite town name because you can say things like:*

"Where'd you have your accident, Sid?"

"Hit an effin' patch of black effin' ice in effin' Effin'ham and slid into the effin' ditch."

Ellsworth

One of the few towns in New Hampshire I've never visited, so I can't say for sure that it exists. But some say it does, in the woods near Wentworth and Campton, and even has its own mountain, Kineo. It's our second-smallest town, population-wise. Eighty-seven souls last count, beat out only by Hart's Location.

Epping

Pronounced Ep-in

Dan Harvey tells about the fella taking the train to Fremont, who got annoyed with the conductor. When the conductor asked where he wanted to go, the fella said, "Go to hell."

The conductor said, "I'll leave you in Epping—that's as close as you'll get."

Fitzwilliam

Sounds fancy, don't it? The village is picture-perfect—nicely preserved town buildings surrounding a neatly kept green in the Monadnock region near Troy. If you want to see a quintessential New Hampshire village, you can't beat Fitzwilliam. It sits 1,200 feet above sea level, one of the highest quintessentials you'll find.

Francestown

Two old friends sat in lawn chairs beside the road waiting for the parade to start. It was a hot, dozy day. After the parade, Fred says to Mick: "That was the longest parade we ever had in Francestown. Three floats! Every other year, there's been just one or two."

Mick says, "Damn fool, there were five floats and a marching band—you slept through most of it."

Franconia

Where the Old Man of the Mountain used to live. Still home to natural wonders like The Basin, The Flume, and Cannon Mountain with its balls.

Franklin

Best town by a dam site. Before 1943, it was the best town by no dam site.

Freedom

The Live Free or Die state would be incomplete without its Freedom.

Check out Old Home Week—end of July, beginning of August. Among the festivities: Ducky Day, when 1,000 rubber duckies take a ride over the millpond dam in town center. The first three duckies to take the plunge win money for the folks who bet on them.

Go, duckies, go.

French Hussey Road

I don't know how this Rochester road earned this name.
P'rhaps you can guess.

Frost Free Library in Marlborough

A warm place to be on a cold morning.

Frying Pan Lane, Stratham

Suggests dramatic marital discord; I could be wrong.

Gonic

Where Gonecians live

Reminds me of my daughter's high school teacher and his
skepticism about the existence of Venetians. She raised her hand.
"Mr. Martel, are you sure you don't believe in Venetians?"

"Absolutely not!"

She's pretty sure he meant "Venusians."

I believe in Gonecians. In fact, I know a couple.

Goose Eye Mountain

In Maine, but you get a good view of it from Berlin's west side

When Rita was a little girl she could see Goose Eye Mountain
out her bedroom window. With the smokestack from the Berlin
Mills placed just so, the mountain appeared to be erupting. She
thought she lived near a volcano.

Gorham

*Sister city to Berlin, though the metropoli share a rivalry; at one time,
for a Berlin boy to date a Gorham girl was considered scandalous—
and vice versa.*

As for the name Gorham, I'm told a fella lived on Cascade Hill
and stored his barrels of homemade liquor near to the top. Along
comes the Hurricane of '38. The trees fall, the house blows right

216

off the side of the hill, and the barrels of liquor appear to be in danger of being dislodged and rolling down the side of the hill.

Villagers at the bottom, hopeful, chanted *Go-rum*, and that's how Gorham, pronounced *Go-rum*, got its name.

Or maybe it was named for Gorham, Maine.

Goshen

Say, "I'm going to Goshen," and somebody's bound to respond: "Land o' Goshen!"

Gunnison Lake, great for canoeing and bird-watching, is fondly known as the Goshen Ocean.

Great Bay

A large saltwater bay and estuary on the seacoast

Years ago Aristotle Onassis wanted to build an oil refinery in Great Bay, and Meldrim Thompson, governor at the time, thought that was a fine idea. Locals disagreed. They fought the rich man and the politician as best they could.

A native owned a house and land in the middle of the plot Onassis needed for his project. Onassis offered the native a lot of money to sell. Some say he turned down a million dollars—and he was not a rich man. When asked why he refused to sell, the native said, "If I sold my house, where would I live?"

The refinery was never built.

Greenland

Small town on the seacoast

Phil sailed his boat down the Piscataqua, under the Sullivan Bridge and into Great Bay. He fell asleep, and when he woke the boat was almost run up on the land. He hollered to a man on the shore, "Where am I?"

"Greenland."

"Oh, my god!"

He thought he'd ended up on that big island in the North Atlantic.

Groveton

Bustling burg near the top of the state

The town cop stopped a car for speeding. "Where are you from?" he asked the driver.

"Pittsburgh," the driver said.

"Don't give me that," the cop said. "I know you're lying. You've got Pennsylvania plates."

Pittsburg, New Hampshire, lies just north of Groveton.

Hart's Location

The smallest town in the state population-wise—40 people, give or take—it prides itself on being First in the Nation every four years, when the voters troop to the polls at midnight and dutifully perform their civic duty and vote in the primaries.

In 2008, John McCain and Sarah Palin got all 10 votes in the Republican primary. On the Democratic side, the Obama/Biden ticket garnered 17 votes, and Ron Paul sneaked in with 2 write-ins. Dixville Notch votes early, too, but they've got more people (75, give or take) so the votes take longer to count. And, technically, they're an unincorporated village—not officially a town. (Don't mention it though—might hurt their feelings.)

Haverhill

Though hilly, it's pronounced Hay-ver-ill; the second H is silent.

Henniker

The only Henniker on earth

Hennikerborough

Years ago, Hillsboro was a dry town; Henniker, however, had a bar.

John Colburn tells the story of Hennikerboro on YouTube, but here's the gist: A fellow, being thirsty, oozed over to Henniker for a couple of drinks. When he got home, his wife asked where he'd been. He started to say Henniker, then switched to Hillsborough midstream. The lie that came out of his mouth was Hennikerborough.

Hill

Home of the flattest downtown in the state

It's flat because the town buildings were moved in 1937 to a nice level spot when the original town center was designated as flood control for the new dam in Franklin.

True fact: In the late 1800s the water for Dr. Vail's famous water cure was drawn from a swamp near Hill village.

Hippie Hill

In Danbury, it's a knoll between the main road and railroad tracks dead center of the village

When I was a kid, in the 1960s, many hippies were to be found on that hill, all times of day and night. Drove by the other day—the hippies are still there! A little grayer, though. Two of them were playing hoss shoes.

Jaffrey

A native of Jaffrey lived most of her adult life in Jasper, Georgia. This transplant received a call from Jasper town hall. They were selling plots in a new cemetery. Would she like to purchase one? She said, "I have a plot in Jaffrey, New Hamsphire, and I can't wait to get there."

Around Halloween, Jaffrey residents decorate with hundreds of scarecrows, all up and down Main Street, in front of McDonald's, the drugstore, the fire station, the police station, the town hall. It's eerie driving through at night—like a crowd of people lining the streets, but nobody moving. Might give a person the willies.

Kensington

When the Seabrook Nuclear Power Plant went online years ago, officials in neighboring Kensington met with officials from the Nuclear Regulatory Commission to discuss evacuation procedures. Charlie Eastman agreed to help out.

The nuclear regulator man said, "Charlie, you're to be the chief contact person."

"Ayuh," Charlie says.

"Say the phone rings, and it's a fella telling you he's at a phone booth at the other end of town and there's a serious problem at the nuclear power plant. What are you going to do?"

"Nuthin'," Charlie says.

"Nothing!"

"There's no phone booth in Kensington."

Laconia

Pronounced by some, including my mother-in-law, Lillian LaPierre Rule, LAY-cone-ee-ah. She pronounced it this way even before she moved up from Conquered.

Each June during bike week, the city fills with motorcycles, snarling traffic for miles around.

Lake Umbagog

Either UM-ba-gog *or* Um-BAY-gog, *depending on whom you talk to, even in the North Country. I find asking people how they pronounce the name of the big shallow lake just south of Canada makes a nice icebreaker. Translated from Abenaki,* Umbagog *means clear water.*

The fella from away was up at the tip of the state on his first ice-fishing expedition. His hosts loaded all the gear—tip-ups, shiners, auger, beer—into the old pickup and drove across the ice toward a likely cove on Umbagog.

The fella noticed a long rope trailing off the back bumper, attached to an empty milk jug, bouncing along the ice as they drove. "What's that for?" he asked.

"That's a flotation marker—so if we go through the ice and sink to the bottom they'll know where to find us."

Lake Winnipesaukee

Biggest lake in the state, 72 square miles of water

When the fella from away first laid eyes on Winnipesaukee, he said: "That's a lot of water."

To which the local replied: "Yup, and that's just the top of it."

Lempster

Land of the silent P

Lyndeborough

At town meeting a person from away kept calling the town Lyndyborough. Finally, the residents rose as one and corrected him. "It's Lineboro."

Manchvegas

Manchester

Ironic reference to how much the Queen City has in common with the gambling mecca in Nevada. That is, not much.

Market Square

In Portsmouth, pronounced Mah-kit Squay-uh

A good place to observe tourists and their antics. Market Square is home to shops, restaurants, bowteeks, the Portsmouth Athenaeum (a grand old museum and library), and more. It's a hive of activity not far from Prescott Park by the sea, full of flow-ers in the summer. Market Square is within walking distance of Strawbery Banke (that's really how you spell it), a living history museum of olde houses you can tour.

Milan

Pronounced as in the folk song, "This lan is your lan, this lan is My-lan"

Monroe

Nestled on the banks of the Connecticut River, this town in northwest-ern New Hampshire may be the source of the old saw, "You can't get they-ah from he-ah," because it's a long twisty ride from all directions. A beautiful ride, though, through woods and farmland with river and mountain views.

Eileen Brown got a lesson in nativity at the Monroe Harvest Festival.

"We had a parade for our Harvest Festival on Saturday morning, and our grand marshal was Bernice Blake, Monroe's oldest living citizen. Even though she is currently living in the Grafton County Nursing Home, there she was, all decked out and ready to wave at the head of our parade. Now, I do not make a habit of asking women their age—especially women of a certain age—but seeing as I was going to write the notes for our parade announcer, I thought we should know just how old our oldest citizen was. Turns out, she is ninety-five and a half. I was very pleased to meet her.

"Immediately after the parade, I was introduced to Les Ward. Les is the founder of Pete & Gerry's Organic Egg Farm here in town, and his daughter, Carol Laflamme, had brought him down to judge the parade. It was quite an honor to meet him. Carol happened to mention that Les was the oldest living citizen in Monroe. Confused, I mentioned I'd just met a woman called Bernice Blake who claimed to be the oldest living citizen. She was ninety-five and a half, I said, and how old was Les? (It's not quite as bad to ask a man his age, I think, as a woman.) 'Ninety-two,' he said proudly. That woman, he said, was not 'native born.' He meant in Monroe. Apparently up here being native born isn't just about New Hampshire born. You have to be town born, too!"

Darned right you do.

Mont Vernon

Don't dare call it Mount, even though Alonzo J. Fogg spelled it "Mount Vernon" in his *Statistics and Gazetteer of New Hampshire*, published in 1874. He got it wrong, according to contemporary historians, who say it's Mont from way back. In fact, they say, in 1853 a hotel owner with political connections thought Mont looked funny. He named his place the Mount Vernon House and lobbied to have the "misspelling" corrected and the name of the town changed to Mount Vernon. This did not sit well with the natives, and the change did not take.

The Mount Vernon House later burned, and that was the end of that discussion.

Mosquito Bridge

Connects Belmont and Tilton over Winnisquam Lake

The original wooden bridge was built in the 1840s, replaced in 1916. The original bridge had a hump in the middle that resembled the back of a mosquito.

It's a well-known local landmark.

Mount Deception

At 3,700 feet, it's bigger than it looks.

223

Mount Moosilauke

If you find yourself at the top of Mount Moosilauke, you're up 4,810 feet, and you've done some substantial climbing. Pronounced *Moos-a-law-key*, the name may mean bald-headed peak, place of ferns, or good place to see moose along the brook, depending on who you ask.

Mount Washington

The highest peak in the Presidential Range of the White Mountains; not to be confused with the Mount Washington, *a cruise ship that slides tourists around Lake Winnipesaukee.*

For a fee (bring your pocketbook—but it's worth it), you can stay at the observatory on top of Mount Washington for a night or two, take a class, learn something about geography, geology, weather, or some other interesting subject, and feel like a bona fide observer. One Christmas I bought my husband, John Rule, a package deal. It involved an overnight stay, some walks around the summit, and a class on geology. In January.

Did I mention that Mount Washington is famous for having the worst weather in the world, especially in January?

No, I wa'n't trying to kill him. Just wanted to give the old man a thrill.

He was pretty thrilled when the two-hour ride up stretched to six on account of the nine-foot snowdrifts. He lucked out though, weatherwise. The day before his adventure the wind at the peak registered 114 miles per hour. The day he arrived the temperature was a toasty four-below and the winds just 53 mph.

Nashua

Second-largest city in the state, behind Manchester; closing in on 88,000 people. Old-timers call it Nash-oo-ay.

Nelson

Home of a long-running contra-dance series, every Monday night, at the Nelson Town Hall, with music by New Hampshire treasures Bob McQuillan, Harvey Tolman, and friends

New Boston

Home to the famous glacial erratic, Frog Rock; big rock, looks just like a frog. Or maybe a toad; it is kind of warty.

Newfound Lake

One of our prettiest, deep and clean

In Hebron they tell of Albert Fogg who surprised townfolks by showing up for town meeting one March. Albert lived across the lake from town hall. He had no car or near neighbors, and it was a long walk around Newfound.

"How'd you get here, Albert?" they asked.

"Walked across the lake."

"How'd you dare to do it, Albert, with the ice so thin and punky?"

"Made myself as light as I could and walked right along fast."

New Hampshire

That's how we spell it, but not how many of us say it. Variations include: New Hampsha, N'Hamsha, and, in the North Country, especially Berlin, New Hampsheer. We're pretty sure nobody much says New Hampshur, except on television.

New London

Home to Colby-Sawyer College and the venerable Barn Playhouse; it has a gazebo on the town common and a skating rink by town hall, putting the picture in picturesque.

In 1959 Ira Littlefield had been water and sewer commissioner in New London since 1904. At town meeting that year, somebody complained that there was no map of the water and sewer lines.

Ira said: "I know where they are."

"What about if you retire, Ira, or, God forbid, if you die. What then?"

"Then," Ira said, "it's not my problem."

Pancake Road, Wilmot Flat
Don't get much flatter than that

Penacook
After the Indian tribe; locals call it Pennycook.

The Hannah Dustin monument, down the hill from the Park and Ride just before the turn to the village, commemorates the young mother from Haverhill, Massachusetts, who killed quite a number of Pennycooks on an island in the Merrimack River after they kidnapped her and killed her children in 1697. The New Hampshire Historical Society sells Hannah Dustin bobbleheads and, in an attempt at political correctness, a Chief Passaconaway bobblehead as well. The political correctness police didn't buy it. The John Stark and Old Man of the Mountain bobbleheads proved much less controversial.

Peyton Place

A fictional town featured in the racy best-seller by Grace Metalious, who lived in Gilmanton when the novel came out in 1956. Folks in Gilmanton are still a little touchy on the subject.

Piermont
A small, lively town over Vermont way

I asked a gathering of Piermont folks for some Piermont stories. Helga said: "Nothin' funny about Piermont."
Somebody else piped up: "Nothing ever happens in Piermont."

Convinced this was an exaggeration, I asked, "What do you do for fun?"

"Pay taxes."

Piscataqua

This tidal river separates Maine from New Hampshire, Kittery from Portsmouth.

It looks smooth and calm, but the currents are very strong and can be dangerous. Piscataqua does not rhyme with Chautauqua. It's got a CAT in the middle of it: *Pis-CAT-a-qua*, from the Abenaki, meaning grumpy swimming cat.

Plaistow

The native said, "It's *Plass-toe,* like in toe, not *Plass-tau,* like in cow."

Her neighbor said, "I say *Plass-tau* like in cow."

The native said, "That's because you've only lived here twenty-five years."

So, it's either *Plass-toe* or *Plass-tau*. I'm not getting into the middle of that one.

Portsmouth

Not pronounced Ports-mouth*, but* Port-smith

Ruth went to college in Maine. Over spring break, she headed home to New Hampshire and invited a couple of friends from school to visit. They were from the Midwest, so the weeklong break didn't give them enough time to make the long trip home worthwhile. She gave them directions to her family home in Portsmouth, but they failed to appear at the appointed time. Around ten at night, she got a call. The friends were lost. They'd tried real hard, but couldn't find Port Smith on the map.

Pull and Be Damned Point

Offshore from the old prison at the Portsmouth Shipyard, where the tidal current is so strong you can row your heart out and make no progress at all.

Rum Hill

In Concord, it's rumored to be the site of a 19th-century picnic in a chestnut grove that turned into a brawl because the picnickers drank too much rum. We don't forget those sorts of transgressions around here. The chestnuts are long gone, but we remember the rum.

Rye Beach

Aunt Minnie from the Midwest always wanted to see the ocean. In her old age she finally got the chance because her nephew was stationed at Pease Air Force Base in Newington. Minnie flew to New Hampshire and her nephew took her to Rye Beach to see the ocean for the first time.

As they stood on the sand looking at the ocean, he noticed that Minnie seemed a little down in the mouth.

"What's the matter, Aunt Minnie?" he said.

"Oh," she said, "I had an idea it would be bigger than this."

Salisbury

With a silent i, it's pronounced Sals-berry; *white church, white town hall, big ole white colonial houses.*

Birthplace of Daniel Webster, except that the part of Salisbury where Webster was born is now considered Franklin, or vice versa.

Seabrook

A seacoast town, home to the Seabrook Nuclear Power plant, but once a fishing village

Legend has it that an early minister loudly credited the settlement of the coast of New Hampshire to God. A local fisherman rose and said: "You mistake us for Massachusetts. They came for God. We came for cod."

Seabrook natives talk differently from anyone else in the state, and many of them trace their roots directly back to England, when their ancestors came across the pond in the 1600s. Linguists study the way Seabrookers talk and say it's kind of like olde English.

Short Falls

In Epsom, it's on a river, but Martin Gross suggests the area might have been inhabited by revenue forecasters.

South Sutton

Holds a good old-fashioned Old Home Day each summer. Residents dress in vintage clothes and gather at the meetinghouse for a brief church service, a speaker, and music. Then there's a picnic and games on the green.

I'm told that for the Fourth of July parade, the people of South Sutton draw straws to see who will march and who will watch.

Squam Lake

There's Big Squam and Little Squam

The movie (based on the play by Ernest Thompson) *On Golden Pond* was filmed on Big Squam. Businesses in the area have adopted the name: The Inn on Golden Pond, The Manor on Golden Pond, Golden Pond Country Store, etc. Locals can even point you to the rock where Henry Fonda's boat got hung up in the movie.

Stump Street

In Candia; sounds like rough going

Swanzey Center

Not to be confused with Center Swanzey, which doesn't exist. I know because once I swapped the words around in a story and was swiftly corrected. Mark, pronounced Maahk, runs a farm stand in Swanzey Center. This story was told to me by Mark's dad, who witnessed the interaction.

A Maine potato farmer was looking over the produce and flowers and such. Mark approached: "Can I help you?"

"Yes," the potato farmer said. "My wife is sick, so I thought I'd buy her a little something to cheer her up."

Mark said, "I think I can help you." He brought out two beautiful blood-red geraniums, heavy-headed, in full bloom, and in clay pots.

"How much?" the potato farmer said.

"These are eight ninety-five a piece."

"She ain't that sick," the farmer said, and bought a flat of petunias for $3.50.

Tadadump Road

In Holderness

This road at one time must have had a dump on it. Maybe still does. I've seen the sign but never took the turn.

Which reminds me of the fellow from away looking for Cilley's Cave in Canaan. He asks the native on the side of the road, "Does this road lead to the trail to Cilley's Cave?"

"Don't know," says the native. "Never been clear to the end."

Tuckerman Ravine

In spring, when the snow has melted most places, there's still plenty in Tuckerman Ravine, a bowl—a glacial cirque—on the side of Mount Washington. Skiers hike in and ski in the bowl.

Unity

Lovely little town near Plainfield

Martha and Paul were in their 70s when they tied the knot. The preacher read the vows: "Repeat after me. I, Paul, vow to live with Martha in peace and unity."

Paul says, "I'll agree to live in peace, but damned if I'll live in Unity."

Warner

Pronounced Wah-nah

My friend, a serious businesswoman, tries to put Rs in where they belong, but some words she just can't seem to master. She said, "I can put the first R in Wahnah, but darned if I can get the second."

I thought, "There's two Rs in Wahnah?"

Weare

Those who live on the north end of town live No. Weare—at least, that's what the sign says.

David Souter is a native of Weare, though he spent a few years in Washington, D.C., on the U.S. Supreme Court. I wonder if, when he traveled home to New Hampshire on break, a conversation like this might have occurred.

"Where you headed?"

"Home."

"Where?"

"Weare."

"Yuh, where?"

231

"I told you, Weare."

"No, you didn't."

"Yes, I did."

"Well then, where?"

"Weare."

Weeks Circle

A traffic circle in Dover where a Weeks Dairy Bar Restaurant used to stand, home of the Weeksie Burger

As a kid, I enjoyed the Weeksie Burger, a hamburger with bacon and relish. The Dairy Bar is long gone, as is the circle, which is now an intersection with traffic lights. Nevertheless, many still give directions that include the Weeks Circle.

"Where do you live?"

"Somersworth, just about a mile east of the Weeks Circle."

Or, "How do I get to the Cozy Nest?"

"We're easy. Diagonally across from Key Auto on Route 108, corner of Blackwater Road. Two miles up from where the Weeks Circle used to be."

Weirs

Called The Weirs or Weirs Beach, a busy summer tourist attraction on Winnipesaukee near Laconia, it's named for weir baskets used by the Winnipiseogee Indians to catch migrating fish.

Each June during bike week, The Weirs is solid with motorcycles. That's when a lot of the locals enjoy their vacations in Maine.

Westmoreland

Pronounced WES-muhlan; *best said fast*

West Wakefield

There is none.

Native Bill Twombley told me why. "Bill," his neighbor Urban said, "there's all kinds of rocks in the ground around my place. Mica, feldspar, quartz, beryl. You better go careful digging. Never know what you're going to find. Nineteen sixty-two, Muhtha got it into her head she wanted an artesian well. Hired the job out, and the workers came in with their big truck and that big old thumpa-thumpa drill. They commenced to drillin'. 'Course, you had to pay by the foot, so the deeper they went, the more it cost you.

"They drilled down about two hundred feet, just a-grinnin', til they hit a pocket of mica. It was soft and the hole caved in on itself. The thumpa-thumpa got buried. They had to bring in derricks, pulleys, earthmovers, and so forth to dig out what was stuck. By gawd, if they didn't drill right into that pocket again and lose that bunch, too.

"It was torrible. They kept bringing in more equipment, bigger equipment, and losing it down the hole, which got bigger and bigger. Pretty soon the bahn slid in. Pretty soon the house slid in. Muhtha and I had to sell off and move out of West Wakefield."

Bill said, "Urban, you tell a lie. There's North, South, and East Wakefield, but no West Wakefield."

Urban said, "Not anymore there isn't. It's all down in the hole."

Wilton

The trouble with Wilton, they say, is you have to keep watering it.

233

Resources

Books

Bailey, Joanne. *A Guide to the History and Old Dwelling Places of Northwood, New Hampshire.* Peter E. Randall Publisher. A thorough town history, full of stories that go all the way back to the 1700s.

Boswell, Mary. *Seasoned with Grace,* The Countryman Press. Stories and recipes from the Shakers. New Hampshire was home to two Shaker villages, one in Canterbury and one in Enfield. Though no more Shakers live in these villages (they were celibate, so this is not unexpected), both have become museums, well worth visiting. Mary Boswell serves as executive director at the Enfield Village.

Botkin, B. A. *A Treasury of New England Folklore,* Crown, 1947. More than 900 pages of real small print, of stories from all over New England going back to before the Revolutionary War.

Chase, Howard N. *Country Piano Tuner: His Stupid Song,* published by the author, 1971. A delightful book of tales recounting Howard's adventures traveling house to house, tuning pianos. Howard's niece, Brenda Wright, gave me a copy with the note: "I hope (and Howard would hope!) that you find some gems to use in your work." I did. And, "You would have delighted in knowing Uncle Zowie." I wish I had.

dePaola, Tomie. *Front Porch Tales & North Country Whoppers,* Penguin, 2007. A collection of classic New England stories, retold for children. Humorous and graced with Tomie's distinctive illustrations. Tomie lives in New London. He's not a New Hampshire native, but he's lived here so long we've adopted him. Or maybe he's adopted us.

Fogg, Alonzo. *The Statistics and Gazetteer of New Hampshire*, D. L. Guernsey Bookseller and Publisher, 1874. A record of old-time New Hampshire.

Gould, John. *Maine Lingo: Boiled Owls, Billdads, & Wazzats*, Down East Books, 1975. Wicked funny and informative. I read it in search of language seepage between New Hampshire and Maine, and, sure enough, found some.

Hall, Donald. *String Too Short to Be Saved: Recollections of Summers on a New England Farm*, Nonpareil Books, 1983. This famous poet writes about his family homestead in Wilmot, where he summered as a child, and where he retired from teaching to write full-time years later.

Haywood, Charles F. *Yankee Dictionary: A Compendium of Useful and Entertaining Expressions Indigenous to New England*, Jackson and Phillips, 1963. Each citation inspires a story or two, which makes for entertaining reading.

Hendrickson, Robert. *Yankee Talk: A Dictionary of New England Expressions*, Castle Books, 2002. Words and expressions from Maine, New Hampshire, and Vermont, with histories of how some originated. I read it cover to cover and came away with the notion that these three states have much in common linguistically.

Hickson, Robert and Mary. *The Place Names of the White Mountains*, Down East Books, 1980. A history of the White Mountains region organized by place names, which makes it easy to find just what you're looking for.

Kreek, Cassandra; Kreek, Emily; Relihan, Ian, editors. *Too Much Water, Too Much Rain: The Story of the Alstead Flood,* Alstead Historical Society, 2006. A collaboration between high school students and the historical society resulted in this collection of first-person stories, pictures, and a timeline of the terrible flood of 2005. A remarkable job of catching history as it unfolded.

Lewis, Gerald E., illustrated by Tim Sample. *How to Talk Yankee*, Thorndike Press, 1979. Pithy, humorous guide to Maine words and pronunciations.

McDonald, John. *Down the Road a Piece: A Storyteller's Guide to Maine,* Islandport Press, 2005. Comical from beginning to end.

McDonald, John. *The Maine Dictionary*, illustrated by Peter Wallace, Commonwealth Editions, 2000.

Tardiff, Olive. *They Paved the Way: A History of New Hampshire Women*, PublishingWorks, 2006. Originally printed in 1960, this collection of essays features 25 prominent women—from accused witches to classical composers—who lived in New Hampshire between 1590 and 1944.

Wetherbee, Fritz. *Speak N'Hampsha Like a Native*, CD available from New Hampshire Movies, www.nhmovies.com, even though it's not a movie. Nobody speaks and knows New Hampshire like Fritz, who tells our story weeknights on *New Hampshire Chronicle*, WMUR, Channel 9. He is also the author of *Fritz Wetherbee's New Hampshire*; *Fritz Wetherbee: Taken for Granite*; *Fritz: More Stories from New Hampshire Chronicle*; and *In Good Company*.

A few helpful websites

amc-nh.org

Activities, events, volunteer opportunities, weather, photos, and a White Mountains guide from the New Hampshire chapter of the Appalachian Mountain Club.

mountwashington.org

News, weather, and a webcam from the top of Mount Washington.

nh.com

Guide to the Granite State. Blogs, maps, activities, where to stay, where to eat. Also history, statistics, geography, and contests. Comprehensive and continuously updated information and commentary for residents as well as tourists.

townofnelson.com

All the facts about Nelson, from the town clerk's hours to back issues of the local paper, the *Grapevine*. You don't see many town websites featuring poetry, but this one does. Also, photo slide shows: Cats of Nelson, Dogs of Nelson, Wildlife of Nelson.

weirsbeach.com

Tourist information and history for Winnipesaukee and surrounds. Loads of photographs, including vintage postcards.

winnipesaukee.com

Statistics on ice-out, webcam live from The Weirs, water temperatures, photos, weather, blogs.

About the Author

Rebecca Rule has lived in New Hampshire all her life (so far). She is a graduate of the University of New Hampshire and taught writing classes there for a number of years. She is the author of *Live Free and Eat Pie! A Storyteller's Guide to New Hampshire*, and three short story collections about New Hampshire, including *The Best Revenge*, named Outstanding Work of Fiction by the New Hampshire Writers' Project. She regularly writes a blog, which can be found at www.livefreeandeatpie.com. She is best known for her live storytelling events, many sponsored by the New Hampshire Humanities Council. She lives in Northwood with her husband, John Rule—who she calls John Rule—and their wire fox terrier, Bob.